Citizen Obedience

THE NATURE OF LEGAL OBLIGATION

BEN WOOD JOHNSON

TESKO PUBLISHING: PENNSYLVANIA

Copyright © 2019 Tesko Publishing Paperback Edition
Copyright © 2014 by Ben Wood Johnson

All rights reserved. No part of this publication may be reproduced, distributed, or transmitted in any form or by any means, including photocopying, recording, or other electronic or mechanical methods, or by any information storage and retrieval system without the prior written permission of the publisher, except in the case of very brief quotations embodied in critical reviews and certain other noncommercial uses permitted by copyright law.

Johnson, Ben Wood
Citizen Obedience: The Nature of Legal Obligation / Ben Wood Johnson.— Tesko Publishing ed.
Includes bibliographical references and index.
ISBN-13: 978-1-948600-08-8 (pbk.)
ISBN-10: 1-948600-08-0

This book was first published in 2019
The information illustrated in this book was compiled for a school project. The analysis is based on class notes and other materials.

Johnson, Ben Wood
Citizen Obedience/The Nature of Legal Obligation
Tesko Publishing website address: www.teskopublishing.com

Eduka Solutions
330 W. Main St. #214
Middletown, PA 17057, USA

Printed in the United States of America

BEN WOOD POST
www.benwoodpost.com
Cover Illustration Nerry Oliver

Ben Wood Johnson, Ph.D.

Author's note: Dear reader, thank you for choosing this book. Although this is a text about legal obligations and legal theory, it is worth noting that I am not a connoisseur in legal matters. This edition was not designed to make such a claim. However, I do not consider myself a neophyte in the domain, although my legal expertise is scarce. Nonetheless, this work is philosophical in nature.

Throughout this papyrus, I share my views of about political obligation as candidly as possible. My criticism of common ideas about citizen obligation is based on my years of observations of the practical nature of citizen obedience. My years have been generously occupied with the investigation of legal matters and theoretical legal principles. In conjunction, I have devoted considerable time to the scholarly pursuit of political obligation.[1]

The fervor with which people approach these issues was a revelation to me. I wanted to bring to the table a unique slant in this discourse. Although my position is fortified with references

---

[1] I am a political scientist by trade. I studied political science, holding a master's degree I the field. My studies of politics centered on political philosophy and foreign relations. Thus, my points of view are not the results of random ideas or uninformed ideals about the subject.

to various works, the book is not a mere echoing of thoughts resonating in the existing literature. I am careful not to present a biased perspective in this discussion.

I sought to offer an authentic point of view within this body of work. But it is essential to recognize the constraints of the book. I remain aware of the disputatious nature of my position.

This edition does not provide an exhaustive review of natural law concepts. I have debated the subject in other literary venues. I recommend the book *Natural Law: Morality and Obedience* to learn more about my take on this topic. Still, this edition was designed to be a concise, but also a comprehensive, assessment of the relevant literature. I encourage you to keep these limitations in mind even after you navigate the manuscript. Despite its shortcomings, this composition introduced an alternative narrative into the present discourse about legal obligations.

ALSO BY BEN WOOD JOHNSON

Sartrean Ethics: (ed.) (2016)
Jean-Paul Sartre and Morality (ed.) (2017)
Forced Out of Vietnam: (ed.) (2017)
Natural Law: (ed.) (2017)
International Law: (ed.) (2018)
Cogito Ergo Philosophus (ed.) (2019)
Postcolonial Africa: (ed.) (2020)
Go Back Where You Came From (ed.) (2020)

Contents

Foreword vii

Acknowledgments.. xi

Introduction 1

Chapter 1: The Term Obligation.................................... 7

Chapter 2: The Nature of Obedience 17

Chapter 3: Citizen Consent... 25

Chapter 4: Theoretical Underpinnings of Obligation 37

Chapter 5: Obligation and God................................... 45

Chapter 6: Uncompromised Obedience 53

Chapter 7: Power of the Law...................................... 61

Chapter 8: Authority of Law Enforcement Officers 69

Chapter 9: The Nature of Fabricated Laws 77

Chapter 10: The Notion of Reason............................. 85

Chapter 11: Natural and Positive Laws....................... 93

Chapter 12: Inherency in Legal Obligation............... 105

Chapter 13: Assessing Natural Law.......................... 109

Chapter 14: A Legal Fissure..................................... 117

Conclusions 127

Bibliography 133

Index 139

Foreword

The law is what we make of it; we are what the law makes of us.
—BWJ, 2015

THE BOOK THAT YOU hold so dear "Citizen Obedience" is based on several essays, which had been compiled decades ago. These papers discussed the topic of jurisprudence and citizen compliance. However, their focus was narrower; they explored the link between law and citizen duty. These essays examined the intricacies of legal theory and political philosophy. They discuss how citizens interact with and respond to laws in their social milieu.

The mentioned works were not just theoretical musings. They were based on extensive research and analysis. The aim was to pass on a deeper understanding of the dynamics of jurisprudence and citizen obedience. This edition remains on a similar trajectory, though it is broader in scope.

In *Citizen Obedience*, readers uncover the complexities of legal systems. They learn about how citizens adhere to the law or deviate from it. The goal is to encourage a genuine debate on the nature of the concept of a social contract, which binds members of society together.

The book *Citizen Obedience* was originally published in 2019 under the same title. But it became vital to amend the text, though this edition is not analytically different from its predecessor. Although the views echoed here piggyback on ideas outlined in previous editions, this revision includes concise treatises on legal obligation and citizen obedience. The book examines ideas debating the influence of natural order on the creation of mechanisms to induce citizen obedience.

The manuscript includes thirteen chapters; they are divided into four sections. While the chapters are brief, they provide a comprehensive, but also succinct, exploration of the subject matter. This approach makes it easy for readers to digest the information presented in the text. The sections serve as guideposts. They establish the framework for the conversation, which helps structure the debate effectively.

The first section discusses the concept of obligation. The second section deals with the evaluation of various philosophical constructs. It includes a deep dive into the concept of morality. Another key focus is rationality. The third section interrogates the construct of natural law, which in doing so, it inspects the notion of positive law. The closing section delineates the importance of prevalent perspectives exploring the nature of civic compliance.

Although this volume may seem modest compared to the treatises typically spotlighted in current literature, it offers significant insights into the debate. The book outlines perspectives echoed by notable legal theorists, including prominent figures, such as John Finnis, John Austin, and H.L.A. Hart. Their popular discourses provide a fresh perspective, which also adds depth and nuance to the ideas outlined in this edition.

Moreover, the book scrutinizes the arguments frequently echoed by other esteemed scholars in political philosophy, including Budziszewski, Raymond Wacks, Brian Bix, and Joseph Raz. It challenges misinformed beliefs about the scope of natural law. The book argues in favor of a comprehensive approach in the debate.

In *Citizen Obedience*, readers will learn about the notion that there is nothing innate about a legal obligation. Instead, citizen compliance is inherently unnatural, thus must be enforced. Obedience, as will be laid bare in the present context, must be induced. However, this adherence is never a choice. Rather, it is always a compulsion.

Obedience, as this essay denotes, must be prompted by, from, and for others. Granted, most people do not perceive obligation through a similar lens. Nonetheless, the task at hand is to help readers conceive the essence of civic compliance from an alternate point of view.

This edition does not advocate for anarchy or lawlessness. Granted, the debate can be marred with controversies. While legal scholars and political theorists have debated the nature of legal compliance, the topic remains obscure. A distant expectation is that this edition will make unanimity in the debate. But it is within a reader's prerogative to accept or to challenge the standpoints commonly reflected in the literature. This papyrus offers the latter approach.

This book is not a mere exercise in intellectual vanity. The views echoed here may be of practical relevance. They may incite readers to perceive the world from a distinct vantage point. It is important for people to understand the nature of their obligation to themselves and to others in a social setting. Citizen obedience must be understood through the lens of both individual and collective responsibilities within the confine of a social context.

The effort placed in concretizing this edition is formidable, if not commendable. It may be a challenge, if not downright impossible, to educate readers about citizen obedience. However, take the book with a grain of salt. A better method is to read this text in its entirety and with an open mind. Such a thorough lecture may allow for a comprehensive grasp of the issues at hand.

Foreword

While *Citizen Obedience* offers a distinct approach to the debate, it is not an unassailable authority on the subject. Opinions vary on the nature of citizen obedience. Still, this work is an effort to contest prevailing narratives.

Be receptive while reading *Citizen Obedience*. This edition shies away from legal verbiage. Irrespective of your familiarity with the law or whether you are an expert in legal doctrines, the book extends its welcome. Also, regardless of your acquaintance with the topic, approach this book with the academic curiosity it deserves. But if you find the text intriguing, consider it a worthy addition to your library. Have a delightful reading experience!

Good reading!
Ben Wood Johnson
Pennsylvania, April 19, 2019

Updated on March 2024

Acknowledgments

AUTHORING THIS BOOK was an enlightening and richly rewarding endeavor. However, I alone could not take credit for this publication. This rendition would not have seen the light of day without significant support. The valuable help, the counsel, and the contributions of various individuals made this edition possible.

It is important to express my appreciation to my dear editor, Den Olive, whose discerning observations, steadfast patience, and professional acumen refined this manuscript into a seamless and polished piece of literature. The diligence you exhibited towards this project and your unwavering pursuit of excellence have left a distinctive imprint on every leaf.

My gratitude towards my dear friend Tom Darce is immense for his generous sharing of knowledge, expertise, and experiences that served as the bedrock of the stories echoed in this edition. I would like to express my acknowledgment to other contributors, including Val and Gaby Vilcin, for their guidance and valuable feedback throughout the research and book-writing process.

It is equally essential to recognize the critical role that Tesko Publishing staff members have played in bringing to light "Citizen Obedience." The design, marketing, and public relations teams, notably Wood Oliv, played a vital role in the completion of this book project. Their professionalism and commitment have helped elevate the manuscript. It has reached the attention of a global readership because of their diligent efforts and creativity. This acknowledgment illustrates the multifaceted nature of publishing a book, particularly where various teams collaborate to create a successful product.

A heartfelt note of thanks to my dear friends and colleagues who extended their support, candid feedback, and a receptive ear throughout this journey. I hold your support and fellowship in high regard. Last, but in no way inferior, my everlasting gratitude is for my family and other relatives for their unending love, understanding, and encouragement.

My deepest appreciation extends to Mynn for her endurance, support, and unlimited inspiration. Thanks for reviewing manuscripts after manuscript until I got it right. Your affection and belief in me have made all the difference, especially during the battle with individuals whose abuse of power and authority seemed insurmountable. To all those who participated in the transformation of "Citizen Obedience" into a reality, I offer my sincere thanks and appreciation. This book is as much a fruit of your efforts as mine.

Keywords: law, morality, reason, natural law, positive law, and political obligation

Introduction

WHAT MAKES UP citizen obedience? This question, though seemingly straightforward, prompts an intricate discourse. An obligation might be perceived as a duty or a mandate. However, the matter holds complexities beyond a superficial comprehension of the notion of obedience, as the concept of citizen obligation leaves room for further exploration.

We may need to delve deeper into the essentiality of the terminology of citizen obedience to clarify the notion. Doing so may help uncover critical lacunae within the existing scholarly literature. The discourse on citizen obedience encompasses more than a simple assertion of a citizen's duty or mandate to act or abstain. Because of the compulsive state of human beingness, it is vital to grasp the roots of legal obligation. It is germane to review the mechanism that might trigger a rational for abstaining to abdicate oneself to the law. While this area of the conversation introduces murkier waters, it may also incite potent emotional reactions.

An antagonistic scheme about the law is not a requisite in the conversation. However, I harbor distinctive peculiarities in the views offered here, which, I expect, might not jibe with your own perspectives. Disagreements with my positions might arise as you immerse yourself in the manuscript. What is clear in this context is the absence of a need to challenge the necessity of law within a social environment.

Certain commentators may consider it superfluous to refer to the reason behind the innate obligation felt by individuals to follow the law. Compliance to the law is nonnegotiable. It is an irrefutable fact.

My argument centers on the following premise: Obedience always negates reason. If a person could reason, then that individual would ineluctably question the need for obedience. The person would deny any demand for obedience that is not based on a rational understanding of the need for such a self-induced obligation or this irrefutably socially imposed duty to be or to refrain the self, at times, others, from being a certain way. Thus, rationality, I contend, would almost undermine citizen obedience.

A rational thinker would investigate any demands for blinded obligation. He would question any requirement that would irrevocably undermine the existence of the need for obedience. He would do so given that obedience requires a complete abdication of one's capacity to reason. Those that instigate a person's adherence to the law often provide the same the reason to question the law, as a law could not be enforced objectively.

While a law, as a legal instrument, can be objective or can be construed objectively, its application or its implementation could never be that way. The construct of obedience does not exist as an immutable edifice. The universal application of citizen obedience is subject to debate. This reality is undeniable, as it incites divergent points of view from scholars, politicians, and civilians alike. The goal in the present dialogue is to scrutinize the essence of obedience, particularly the responsibility of each citizen for the laws of the land in which they live.

A pressing need arises to explore the scope of synthetic laws or positive laws, accompanied by an imperative to investigate the ramifications of such legislations. The necessity of this approach requires us to examine the repercussions of noncompliance with artificially instituted laws. We must reassess the implications of overlooking the reality of human existence. The vast majority might struggle to obey artificial laws. However, such refusal might lead to disastrous outcomes, which may help underscore the constant requirement for legal compliance.

The call to probe the scope of artificial laws is pressing. It is important to investigate human reactions towards such laws. It is also fitting to examine the impact of specific legal doctrines in a more approving way. The necessity of reviewing these principles outside the confines of a social setting is also of significance.

There is a need for a rudimentary examination of the term "obligation" in our current context. Yet, I will not venture into extensive depths in the present literary framework.[1] But I might still outline potential interpretation(s) of "natural law." It is important to evaluate the role of authority in engendering citizen obligation. We must understand how authority influences the sense of responsibility among citizens. Assessing the extent of specific authorities is vital, especially in enforcing citizen compliance. It is important to consider the role of government bodies in ensuring that citizens follow rules and regulations. We need to measure their extent of influence and effectiveness.

I could invoke several scenarios to illustrate the essentiality of the issues surrounding the relationship between the citizenry and the laws, which implicate their obedience thereof. Such setups detail the nature of police authority and law enforcement. In the current analytical setting, these scenarios focus on how police authorities often use their power to enforce obedience. I will examine how these entities induce citizen compliance. I will explore how calls to uphold citizen rights often encumber, if not conflict, with the notion of human freedom. However, my

---

[1] Refer to my other works on the subject if you would like to learn more. The manuscript lists them toward the end.

examination of authority is strictly within the boundaries of legal obligation.

Contrasting the concept of positive law with natural law could be beneficial. Developing a systemic explanation for why the laws of nature impose no inherent duty (or intrinsic obligation) upon individuals could be a potential approach. There is a need to understand a natural law as a positive law currently. I will make the case that people perceive the laws of nature, as currently understood, as a divine law (or God's law).

Countering the belief that all men are inherently docile or submissive might be appropriate. Men, by nature, are wavering in their world. That is to say that men are afraid of their own self. Their fundamental nature is ferocious. This has led to certain assertions. The belief that people-made men are destructive entities is one of these. The assertion that men are inherently malleable entities might be an invention.

Men can exhibit behavior that others may interpret as docility. Yet, such malleability, echoing here as well, is a virtue in a minority of men. Only a few achieve this level of self-control. However, there cannot be inherent legal obedience. This worldview may also contravene human nature.

No one is born in preordained obedience to another. No individual is born to submit to any entity or person who has power over them. Men must perpetually obligate themselves. Otherwise, they must induce an obligation in themselves at perpetuity. Then, citizen compliance is inherently coercive.

Granted, the previous statement is not absolute. You might disagree with the above assertion. However, before you challenge my taxation of the nature of citizen obligation, allow me to expand upon this declaration further.

Section 1

Natural Obedience

CHAPTER 1

The Term Obligation

The term "obligation" can be defined in various contexts, notably psychology, business, law, and technology. For example, in the realm of psychological contracts, obligations can stem from formal or implied agreements between parties, as well as perceived obligations that arise through implicit means.[1] These obligations are intertwined with commitments made by the involved parties.[2] Moreover, obligations can be expressed through logic constructs, enabling statements like "individual I has the obligation to see to it that ϕ."[3]

---

[1] Elizabeth Wolfe Morrison and Sandra L Robinson, "When Employees Feel Betrayed: A Model of How Psychological Contract Violation Develops," *Academy of Management Review* 22, no. 1 (1997): 226–56.

[2] Manuel Hilty, David Basin, and Alexander Pretschner, "On Obligations" (Computer Security–ESORICS 2005: 10th European Symposium on Research in Computer Security, Milan, Italy, September 12-14, 2005. Proceedings 10, Springer, 2005), 98–117.

[3] Lambèr Royakkers and Jesse Hughes, "Blame It on Me," *Journal of Philosophical Logic* 49, no. 2 (2020): 315–49.

Chapter 1: The Term Obligation

In the corporate world, the concept of obligation has evolved from a focus solely on profit generation to encompass a broader set of responsibilities, including the generation of shared values.[4] Similarly, in the healthcare sector, obligations are classified into categories such as "must," "should," or "consider," indicating the level of expectation for clinicians to adhere to specific recommendations.[5]

From a legal perspective, obligations play a crucial role in defining responsibilities and entitlements. Effective investigation is highlighted as a valid legal basis for human rights protection, emphasizing the entitlement to public participation.[6] Furthermore, minimum core obligations in international law lack specificity regarding which health services should be included and the obligations of wealthier nations to assist poorer ones.[7]

In computer science and policy frameworks, obligations are integral components. They are often linked to access control

---

[4] Mauricio Andrés Latapí Agudelo, Lára Jóhannsdóttir, and Brynhildur Davídsdóttir, "A Literature Review of the History and Evolution of Corporate Social Responsibility," *International Journal of Corporate Social Responsibility* 4, no. 1 (2019): 1–23.

[5] Jeremy J Michel, Eileen Erinoff, and Amy Y Tsou, "More Guidelines than States: Variations in US Lead Screening and Management Guidance and Impacts on Shareable CDS Development," *BMC Public Health* 20 (2020): 1–10.

[6] Pavel Kotlán, Alena Kozlová, and Zuzana Machová, "Opening a Path towards Sustainable Corporate Behaviour: Public Participation in Criminal Environmental Proceedings," *Sustainability* 13, no. 14 (2021): 7886.

[7] Lisa Forman et al., "What Could a Strengthened Right to Health Bring to the Post-2015 Health Development Agenda?: Interrogating the Role of the Minimum Core Concept in Advancing Essential Global Health Needs," *BMC International Health and Human Rights* 13 (2013): 1–11.

decisions in systems [8] and are declared as soft constraints regulating what is prohibited, permitted, or obliged within distributed systems. [9] Moreover, obligations are specified independently and are referenced in policy definitions.[10]

Obligations encompass commitments, responsibilities, and expectations across various domains, including psychology, corporate governance, healthcare, law, and computer science. They define the duties and constraints that individuals or entities are bound to fulfill, shaping interactions, decision-making processes, and legal frameworks.

Given out focus here is the law, it is worthy of noted that many legal treatises and doctrines have endeavored to rationalize the existence of law, which, consequentially, epitomize or seek to solidify understandings about the term obligation itself.

The term "obligation," particularly in the context of law, embodies a complexity often overlooked. When it comes to the concept of law, the notion is far from concrete and far from immutable. Nebulous legal principles that offer little to no elucidation often form the construct of obligation. These principles, I contend here, do not explain why a law should force a citizen to conform. The mere fact that compulsion must be a

---

[8] Daniel J Dougherty, Kathi Fisler, and Shriram Krishnamurthi, "Obligations and Their Interaction with Programs" (Computer Security–ESORICS 2007: 12th European Symposium On Research In Computer Security, Dresden, Germany, September 24—26, 2007. Proceedings 12, Springer, 2007), 375–89.

[9] Murat Sensoy et al., "OWL-POLAR: A Framework for Semantic Policy Representation and Reasoning," *Journal of Web Semantics* 12 (2012): 148–60.

[10] Mario Lischka, "Dynamic Obligation Specification and Negotiation" (2010 IEEE Network Operations and Management Symposium-NOMS 2010, IEEE, 2010), 155–62.

part of the fundamental existence of laws implies that laws themselves are not a conduct inducer. Rather, there ought to exist specific mechanisms designed to induce legal obedience.

Implications of Legal Obedience

Are there implications, whether good or bad, for legal obedience? The answer is certainly in the affirmative. Legal obedience plays a crucial role across various disciplines. In the field of sociology of law, for instance, compliance with legal rules is essential for determining the effectiveness or failure of these rules.[11] The efficacy of laws and regulations in general heavily depends on public confidence in their effectiveness.[12] This efficacy is also governed by the self-enforced obedience and respect for the rules by those under their governance.[13] In this case, the citizen must not only self-imposed the obligation that stems from the law, but they must also respect and adhere to the rules, which emanated from the said laws or legal principles. In that respect, legal obedience can be classified as physical obedience when citizens are compelled to obey by the state's authority.[14] It can also be

---

[11] Jiangnan Zhu, Huang Huang, and Dong Zhang, "'Big Tigers, Big Data': Learning Social Reactions to China's Anticorruption Campaign through Online Feedback," *Public Administration Review* 79, no. 4 (2019): 500–513.

[12] WP Djatmiko, Suteki Suteki, and Nyoman Putra Jaya, "Reconstruction Legal Culture of Madurese Based on Pancasila Values as Criminal Policy in Tackling Carol," 2019.

[13] Ibid.

[14] Kathryne M Young, "Everyone Knows the Game: Legal Consciousness in the Hawaiian Cockfight," *Law & Society Review* 48, no. 3 (2014): 499–530.

understood as psychological, if not mental, obedience, when citizens self-imposed the obligation to the law itself.

From a psychological standpoint, research has shown that perceived police legitimacy can enhance legal compliance and cooperation with legal authorities.[15] This may impact behaviors, such as voluntary witness cooperation,[16] which can be with law enforcers or with law enforcement entities in general. Additionally, both theoretical and empirical studies emphasize the significance of procedural justice in promoting general cooperation with the law, police empowerment, obedience to legal directives, and overall compliance with legal norms.[17]

In the realm of political philosophy, the concept of legal obedience is closely linked to the idea of political obligation, as will be discussed toward the end of the text with prominent thinkers, including Joseph Raz, H.L.A. Hart, and Leslie Green, to name a few. Granted, the presumption is that in just political communities, the majority of citizens believe they have a moral obligation to obey the law.[18] They view the law as a way to endorse justice and to support just institutions.[19] However, some observers argue that obedience to the law may not be enough.[20]

---

[15] Megan Bears Augustyn, "Updating Perceptions of (in) Justice," *Journal of Research in Crime and Delinquency* 53, no. 2 (2016): 255–86.

[16] Ibid.

[17] Mark C Murphy, "Philosophical Anarchisms, Moral and Epistemological," *Canadian Journal of Law & Jurisprudence* 20, no. 1 (2007): 95–111.

[18] Kevin Walton, "The Particularities of Legitimacy: John Simmons on Political Obligation," *Ratio Juris* 26, no. 1 (2013): 1–15.

[19] Ibid.

[20] Lijun Wei, "Construction of the Interactive Relationship between Law Enforcement and Legislation Based on the Background of Big

Chapter 1: The Term Obligation

It may not lead to stability, efficiency, or justice of a nearly just institutional structure.[21]

The common belief is that the law is supreme. Yet, the fundamental essence of what law is often eludes even the most adept legal minds. Since antiquity, philosophers, moralists, and various intellectuals have grappled with the question of why we should uphold legal principles. The predicament is that misconstrued beliefs about the world often underpin many of these principles. Often, certain legal precepts distort human reality.

Historical analysis demonstrates that long-term obedience of the majority cannot be sustained solely through oppressive imperial politics. This reality underscores the intricate relationship between legal enforcement, societal norms, and the intrinsic motivations that drive individuals to comply with legal mandates. Nonetheless, the argument could be made that legal obedience is a multifaceted concept that influences societal order, governance effectiveness, individual behaviors, and perceptions of justice. Understanding the implications of legal obedience is crucial for policymakers, legal scholars, and practitioners to uphold the legitimacy and efficacy of legal systems.

There are those who passionately believe that obligation is an inherent characteristic of man. The belief in this context is that all individuals inherently obey the law. Nonetheless, I find myself at odds with this point of view. Then, I ask: are human beings predisposed to obey the law?

Data," *Mathematical Problems in Engineering* 2022 (May 17, 2022): e6888268, https://doi.org/10.1155/2022/6888268.

[21] Ibid.

Natural Inclination for Obedience

The question posed in the previous paragraph is intriguing. This pertinent inquiry demands its own venue or its own space for a worthy intellectual debate. To ask such a question is to put into question the rationality of legal obligation in it most intrinsic sense. But for now, let us consider facets of the literature, which echo the sentiment that human beings exhibit a complex relationship with legal obedience, influenced by a range of factors. The current literary discourse has framed the debate in no uncertain terms.

Social scientists studying legal compliance emphasize that individuals generally adhere to the law to the extent that they perceive it and legal actors as authoritative and legitimate.[22] This perception of legitimacy plays a significant role in shaping individuals' willingness to obey the law voluntarily. In the same way, the duty to obey the law can arise from individuals' natural duty to promote social peace, highlighting a moral obligation to adhere to legal norms.[23]

Psychological factors play a role in individuals' propensity to obey the law. Research suggests that perceived police legitimacy can enhance legal compliance and cooperation with legal

---

[22] Richard H. McAdams and Janice Nadler, "Coordinating in the Shadow of the Law: Two Contextualized Tests of the Focal Point Theory of Legal Compliance," *Law & Society Review* 42, no. 4 (December 2008): 865–98, https://doi.org/10.1111/j.1540-5893.2008.00361.x.

[23] John Hasnas, "Is There a Moral Duty to Obey the Law?," *Social Philosophy and Policy* 30, no. 1–2 (January 2013): 450–79, https://doi.org/10.1017/S0265052513000216.

Chapter 1: The Term Obligation

authorities, impacting behaviors such as witness cooperation.[24] That is to say, the concept of procedural justice is crucial in promoting general cooperation with the law, obedience to legal directives, and overall compliance with legal norms.[25]

From a philosophical perspective, the idea of legal obedience is intertwined with the concept of political obligation. As outlined earlier, in political communities where members consider themselves just or righteously befitting, many individuals believe they have a moral obligation to obey the law. Doing so is a means to promote justice and to support the continuity of the just institutions,[26] which serve as the epitome of the social milieu itself. However, some argue that obedience to the law may not be a panacea for social stability and the maintenance of just institutional structures.[27]

My aim is not to refute the notion that obedience is a part of human existence. The human nature is built for compliance. However, facets of the human nature were also designed for

---

[24] Benjamin Oosterhoff et al., "Differential and Domain-Specific Associations Among Right-Wing Authoritarianism, Social Dominance Orientation, and Adolescent Delinquency," *Personality and Social Psychology Bulletin*, June 22, 2017, https://doi.org/10.1177/0146167217711937.

[25] Shuai Wu et al., "Research on Sentiment Analysis of Public Opinion Events Based on Human Behavior Dynamics," vol. 12260 (International Conference on Computer Application and Information Security (ICCAIS 2021), SPIE, 2022), 541–49.

[26] Alexei Sergeyevich Guryanov, Elina Borisovna Minnullina, and Alfred Ildarovich Shakirov, "Kantian Ethics: The Phenomena Of Respect And Worth (Worthiness)," 2021, 675–82, https://doi.org/10.15405/epsbs.2021.11.89.

[27] Yaron Meirovitch et al., "Alpha and Beta Band Event-Related Desynchronization Reflects Kinematic Regularities," *Journal of Neuroscience* 35, no. 4 (2015): 1627–37.

autonomy. Therefore, the argument could be made that human beings' predisposition to obey the law (or not to do the same) can be influenced by a combination of factors, including perceptions of legitimacy, moral obligations, psychological considerations, and philosophical beliefs. Understanding these complexities is essential for policymakers, legal scholars, and practitioners seeking to promote legal compliance and uphold the legitimacy of legal systems.

Here, I hope to infuse a philosophical approach in the debate. It is important to grasp the fundamental sense of legal obligation. A discussion of manufactured laws cannot occur without acknowledging the perceived role of divinity (or God) in crafting those laws. This happens because dogmatic beliefs often lead to some of the most prevalent misconceptions about law. People often defend assertions that bolster any semblance of obedience in men on the grounds of morality or human virtue.

Chapter 1: The Term Obligation

CHAPTER 2

The Nature of Obedience

Nature does not impart a duty beyond its own purview. The natural environment is not punitive. The call of the natural sphere does not compel adherence to laws. People construct these laws artificially or outside the natural environment itself.

Although nature places no fetters upon its creations, it is a mistaken assumption to view humans, at least as constituents of nature, as innately unbound. They do not exist as unconstrained beings within the realm of nature. Authentic liberty eludes them. Yet, even within the parameters of nature, the essential core of human beings remains unshackled.

It is not an inherent decree of nature that humans behave in a prescribed manner. A perpetual quest for freedom is a human trait. From what or who must man seek this liberation? This is a question of captivating interest to which I have devoted a great deal of intellectual, if not mental, stamina.

Natural laws or inherent limitations do not encumber humans in opposition to their fundamental selves. What is natural could not be prohibited. Naturality is inevitability. There are no inherent obligations in the natural. No one is obliged to be who they are or how they are. Obligation, at its core meaning, implies

Chapter 2: The Nature of Obedience

an unnatural state, which must be imposed and/or superposed. Hence, the obligation to that way could never be natural. It must be enforced and reinforced.

Nature does not stand against the natural order of existence, be it human or else. Hence, humans are not naturally subservient to the laws of their own devising. This verity remains actual, regardless of whether divinity sanctifies manmade laws. The same is true whether the origins of said laws are entrenched in fairness or notions of equity. For example, there is no innate obligation for an individual to embody a particular personality or to exist in the world a certain way. Being is an intrinsic state, which could never be modified based on capricious understandings about whom a person is or who that individual should be. Therefore, obligation is always an unnatural state of being and/or existing in the world.

The logical question is why people feel a duty to be a certain way? Why are some people determined to force others to be a certain way? I am not sure of the reason for such a paternalistic worldview or for such a hegemonic attitude towards one's kind. I am not sure why some individuals have given themselves a duty to make others view the world from their prism, which, many a time, is depressingly distorted.

The concept of duty does not find its genesis within nature. As such, it cannot resist objective scrutiny. Such ideologies, which I intend to explain further in this treatise, can only be engaged from a positive standpoint or from a posited rational. Nature, to echo, does not impose itself on a being. It persuades, if not compels, the entity to compel the self to its own nature.

Conformity is not an instinct of humanity. Humans must enforce any obligation towards laws that they themselves have planned. They must also enforce any laws they themselves have interpreted to be a certain way and not the other way around.

They must do this, many a time, under duress. In the absence of such pressure to be this way or that way, such laws would find no adherence, at least not willingly, from the individual who imposed the duty nor from the one such a duty is expected or obliged.

There is a delicate demarcation between doctrinal convictions and similar deductions. They often derive from empirical facts. Convictions demand faith, whereas deduction requires logic and rationality. Likewise, faith, the manifestation of conviction, often stands in stark contrast to tangible knowledge, which can be based on rationality or sequence of logical thinking. Accordingly, an individual's beliefs rarely reflect the level of knowledge that the person may hold or the paucity thereof. The more a person's understanding of the world is based on faith, the more irrational than individual's worldview might be, which could have dire consequences for those around that person.

In a sphere where objectivity reigns supreme, any perspective anchored solely in a system of beliefs would fundamentally challenge the essence of knowledge. The boundary between the world as we perceive it and the world as it exists (or has the potential to exist), remains tenuous. Traditions, conventions, and worldviews do not faithfully represent the world in its actual state or in its potential form. Jurisprudential doctrines are rooted in perceptions and understandings of the world. However, the merits of such doctrines can be contingent on specific temporal and spatial contexts, making them whimsical tools to induce social compliance.

The perspectives unveiled here may seem fragmented. Readers may perceive my views as obstinate. However, this work does not hinge on a myopic understanding of the matters at hand. The same, it does not provide haphazard opinions on the prevalence or pertinence of human jurisprudence.

Chapter 2: The Nature of Obedience

Prone to Obedience

How can we reconcile obedience with the innate state of human existence? Laws serve as mechanisms of control, which can be social or psychological in nature. By contrast, the essence of humanity runs counter to any notion of constraint.

Intrinsically, humans are intended for freedom; or at the least, they are destined to pursue freedom relentlessly and ceaselessly within the bounds of their understanding of their circumstances or isolation. This pursuit forms the essence of their reality. It infuses in them a life with purpose, which often drives them to realize a self beyond the event of their world.

The connection between obligation and obedience is not one born of nature. From the stat of their existence, no individual exhibits a natural predisposition to legal obedience. Obedience is a manufactured state. The inclination of most people is to disregard any obedience which lacks an organic genesis; the law is no exception to this.

Despite the pervious proclamations, human existence unfolds within legally constructed environments. This idea implies that humans are inherently designed to comply; they must do so actively and relentlessly. Is this an accurate depiction?

What could lead an individual to obey the law? The responses are as varied as the individuals themselves. It becomes necessary to examine to what extent a person might feel compelled to submit to the rules or the authority of others. This submission occurs regardless of the perceived injustice, ambiguity, or potential harm that such authority may present.

The concern for the individual's well-being adds complexity to the problem. Understanding this dynamic can inform discussions about personal autonomy, social structures, and ethical considerations surrounding obedience to authority. It opens avenues for further study and contemplation in the legal, sociological, and psychological domains.

Humans are adrift in their world; they are engaged in a ceaseless quest for meaning. They exhibit an inherent irresoluteness about their reality. New interpretations about the nature of humanness are constantly being invented, making the human reality more unsettled. These interpretations often relate to the incomprehensible aspects of their existence. They are inclined to devise methods and methodologies to rationalize circumstances beyond their comprehension. Such is the reality of humans in their world.

We cannot ignore the paradox of human existence. We envision law as a guide for humanity; it is an instrument intended to instill a sense of certainty. It serves as a tool for providing the assurance of predictability within the human world.

Despite centuries of legal reliance on behavioral regulation, humans remain unsure of their world. They lack clarity about their place in the natural world. They exist within the cosmos unpredictably.

The Fickleness of Men

Human unpredictability echoes through the universe. It shapes laws that reflect this inherent mutability. This complexity renders manufactured laws tangential to the overarching reality of men. This fact exposes the dissonance between artificially constructed laws and the immutable laws of nature.

Synthetic laws are always transient. They devise in tandem with the fluctuating realities of human existence. However, the intrinsic nature of humanity has remained unchanged since its inception.

Chapter 2: The Nature of Obedience

It is undeniable that men harbor uncertainty about their self-identity. The same is true for their understanding of the world where they evolved and their place within it. They wrestle with their role in both social and natural environments. We envisage laws to provide answers to unanswered questions. They serve as a roadmap for men. They create order in a chaotic world.

Artificial laws inherently seek to impose social order. However, these laws remain fragmented and disjointed. They often cannot encapsulate the intricacies of human reality. People often perceive laws as unjust; a reason for that belief is the inherent contrived attributes of laws or their application.

Manufactured laws can be capricious tools of repression. They can function in ways that are not always fair or just. Often, they serve as instruments of oppression. They are frequently invoked to justify unfairness and sustained disparities.

Human laws provoke inquiries about our existence. They often incite questions about their applicability, especially outside the confines of nature. Hence, synthetic laws are always subject to exceptions. As a result, as well, they always carry unpredictability.

In contrast, the laws of nature are ubiquitous. Their impact is tangible. Therefore, no one can revoke such laws, replace them conspicuously, or make them redundant to a point of irrelevance.

Natural laws do not require enforcement. They are free from oppression, suppression, and capriciousness. Their relevance does not hinge on human upholding. All laws derived from nature embody justice, for nature is inherently devoid of unfairness.

Fabricated laws mirror human nature. These laws are arbitrary; they are transient; they are potentially inhumane. Their implementation is always capricious. Manufactured laws reflect the presumptive nature of humans within a world that they have yet to grasp fully.

Artificial laws consistently breed injustice and unfairness. They inspire cruelty, instill fear, and embody immorality and despotism at their core. Despite their ephemeral nature, their effects can cast long-lasting shadows.

Holders of the Truth

It is an inflated self-perception for men to envisage themselves as custodians of human virtue. In a show of hubris, men ascend, or perhaps have placed themselves, to the stature of demigods. They do so with such audacity and boldness that it is almost breathtaking. In the process, they end up usurping the divine title. Laws function as instruments, giving men a veneer of moral justification to undertake immoral deeds. Laws enable men to rise to an imagined plateau of absolute truth.

Men draft their own rules only to shatter them at will. They enforce these self-defined rules selectively. They invoke the name of the Divine to rationalize their legal paradoxes. Men may also allude to nature to rationalize their rules. This is the quintessence of man's absurdity.

Another reality is worthy of note. Men acknowledge their superficiality; they realize the need to justify their actions to mitigate adverse reactions. The law metamorphoses into a mechanism inducing compliance, with obedience coerced through brute force or the looming threat thereof.

How then, faced with their intrinsic uncertainty about their own existence, can men exude such confidence in the world? What prompts men to fabricate laws that, in their estimation,

Chapter 2: The Nature of Obedience

mimic nature? Conclusive answers might be hard to find. Even so, there is an alternative path.

This book investigates the preceding questions as part of a broader intellectual exploration. In the same way, addressing these inquires conclusively might be too complex for the task at hand. Nonetheless, the present edition has sought to lay the foundation for future investigations into the nature of human nature.

Fundamental questions about men remain nebulous; the literature does not offer straightforward solutions. It would be presumptuous to assert that this book alone could decipher the enigma of humankind. Of course, the perspectives presented in this context may provide clarity.

This work centers on the issue of obedience. The primary focus is on examining the legal implications. The principal subject, which I delve into in this papyrus, is citizen obedience. To pave the way for this discourse, let me echo the viewpoints that we shall explore in subsequent chapters.

CHAPTER 3

Citizen Consent

Conceptions about the practical dimensions of natural law remain unsettled. Approaches often stem from a misguided worldview or mistaken assumptions. While the pervading belief is that positive law is of divine origins,[1] people often examine the term natural law from a morality standpoint, for the concept emanated from moral theory.[2] However, the concept itself, both from a theoretical and practical lens, is flawed.[3]

The prevalent consensus among legal intellectuals suggests a stark demarcation between man-made laws and natural laws. However, if such a partition exists, the error might steep it. One could argue the idea of a universal percept, which probes that

---

[1] Constance Youngwon Lee, "Calvinist Natural Law and the Ultimate Good,"," *The Western Australian Jurist* 5 (2014): 153–75.

[2] Russell Hittinger, "Liberalism and the American Natural Law Tradition," *Wake Forest L. Rev.* 25 (1990): 429.

[3] Ibid.

human rights have stemmed from natural concepts[4] might be flawed at its core meaning.

There is a pressing requirement to assess existing misconceptions about the origins of the laws of nature. But a person must make this assessment from a critical lens. It is critical to examine these common misgivings to provide a more accurate understanding. The discovery of misconceptions about laws (or laws recognized as nature) is not a far-fetched view. There are "heavenly errors" about what we consider the actual nature of the universe.[5] There are questions about the origins of the matter within[6] the walls of what we perceive as nature.

Exploring misinterpretations about the laws that men devise is equally imperative. Men inspire these laws based on their understand of whom and where God is located. A coherent understanding of both concepts is integral, particularly in the context of their implications on citizen obedience. We briefly delve into the concept of citizen consent.

A widespread assumption suggests that individuals are predisposed to comply. They are likely to obey. They are prone to obedience. In short, people, even criminals, are likely to obey the law, particularly when considering the influence of legitimacy and social networks.[7] This view is based on the belief that people

---

[4] Catherine Shelley and Catherine Shelley, "Natural Law, Reason and Religion," *Ethical Exploration in a Multifaith Society*, 2017, 59–91.

[5] Neil F Comins, *Heavenly Errors: Misconceptions about the Real Nature of the Universe* (Columbia University Press, 2001).

[6] Emma G Todd, *Discoveries of Misconceptions Regarding the Properties of Matter Within the Science of Chemistry* (Whitaker & Ray Company, 1898).

[7] Adrew V Papachritos, Tracey L Meares, and Jeffrey Fagan, "Why Do Criminals Obey the Law-the Influence of Legitimacy and Social Networks on Active Gun Offenders," *J. Crim. L. & Criminology* 102 (2012): 397.

are predisposed to respond to authority.[8] People believe that the average reasonable person would naturally gravitate towards doing the right thing. Commonly, people consider obeying the law to be the right course of action. As a corollary, we expect a reasonable person to comply with the law. However, this line of reasoning calls for an alternative perspective.

I would argue that the notion of citizen consent is nebulous at best. It is a concept that eludes empirical validation beyond its mere manifestation in social settings. If a citizen exists strictly within a social environment, then we must derive any concept of consent from this framework. This consent, I contend, would amount to nothing. This form of consent should be void. It lies beyond the purview of the natural.

We cannot assume that a citizen consents to society's rules just because he or she is a part of the social milieu itself. The crux lies in mental harmony. This reflects the individual's knowledge. It relates notably to the implications of societal participation. This concept finds resonance in legal circles, often referred to as a "meeting of the minds," which is an informal agreement and social norms.[9]

Within this paradigm, consent to any agreement must be unequivocal. Parties entering an agreement must clearly understand the nature of the agreement and its potential implications. The genesis of any agreement requires consensus that precedes the actual agreement of the parties.

---

[8] Stanley Milgram and Christian Gudehus, "Obedience to Authority," 1978.

[9] Erin L. Krupka, Stephen Leider, and Ming Jiang, "A Meeting of the Minds: Informal Agreements and Social Norms," *Management Science*, May 31, 2016, https://doi.org/10.1287/mnsc.2016.2429.

This perspective on consent is far from whimsical. It finds support in several legal systems. Even the bedrock of contract law substantiates this understanding.[10]

The prevailing sentiment almost expects that obedience will override any sense of self in a person. One might naturally question the reason for this belief. The commonly proposed answer suggests that the individuals have proactively agreed to this obedience. This line of argument is frequently repeated in legal discourse.

The previous logic is intriguing. One might assert that an idealistic perspective predicates any consent that transcends a formal agreement. You can withdraw this consent, as it is transitory. There are conditions that can nullify consent.[11] For instance, we do not consider normative consent as true consent.[12] Likewise, a violation may make a consent ineffective,[13] thereby rendering the content itself null or unenforceable. People may

---

[10] It could be said that every contractual agreement requires a mutual understanding of what must be agreed upon and the consequences of such an agreement. There ought to be a mutual assent. This concept is often described as the meeting of the minds in contract law. There is no such understanding in a social contract. Therefore, a *social contract*, so-called, is an *arbitrary obligation* certain members of society may place on others.

[11] David Estlund, "Political Authority and the Tyranny of Non-Consent," *Philosophical Issues* 15 (2005): 351–67.

[12] Neil C Manson, "Normative Consent Is Not Consent," *Cambridge Quarterly of Healthcare Ethics* 22, no. 1 (2013): 33–44; Ben Saunders, "Normative Consent and Opt-out Organ Donation," *Journal of Medical Ethics* 36, no. 2 (2010): 84–87.

[13] Keith Hyams, "When Consent Doesn't Work: A Rights-Based Case for Limits to Consent's Capacity to Legitimise," *Journal of Moral Philosophy* 8, no. 1 (2011): 110–38.

change their mind; they may nullify any form of consent they have previously entered.

Consent is the unambiguous acknowledgment of an indisputable state of being within the world. It must be a palpable truth. It encapsulates the de facto reality with which the individual must reconcile. Therefore, in every human interaction, consent, by any measure, is indisputable; in the same way, there is always consent or it is always assumed to exist or to have existed.

When one gives consent, it represents an acceptance of the prevailing reality. By doing so, one relinquishes the right to dispute this reality. It involves surrendering to a person's right to reject this reality. It equates to renouncing any opportunity to deny this reality. One has aligned himself with the reality that presents itself.

A law is an entity that does not seek consent. It possesses intrinsic capriciousness. The existence of a law, in and of itself, cannot elicit a sense of duty from an entity that enjoys freedom and independence.

A law possesses an inherent absoluteness. Its existence towers above everything else. It also eclipses any preceding laws. In its most rudimentary form, a law does not require consent from the entities or individuals who are or may become subject to it. Next, we examine the extent to which both manufactured and natural laws foster similar levels of obedience in individuals.

Obedience and Conformity

Several observers perceive obedience as a response to mankind's desire to transcend their natural state. It could also be seen as a reaction to their pursuit of perfection. It may serve as a mirror, which reflects our state of inherent imperfection. It is a constant reminder of our shortcomings and flaws.

The notion that men must show obedience to one another is prevalent. This, some argue, can be a path towards wisdom. For example, acceptance of others' will [is] often touted as a hallmark of wisdom. In this vein, obedience might be asserted to show psychological maturation.

Many argue that obedience opens the door to a state of purity, both mentally and physically. The ability to accept the inevitable, to accept what cannot be altered, is perceived as such. There is a commonly held belief that obedience equates to strength, a culmination of humanity's quest for answers in a world filled with questions that escape understanding. However, this interpretation is not entirely accurate.

Synthetic laws may provide a sense of self to humanity. They may offer individuals a feeling of significance within the natural world. They may help establish a framework for social interaction.

A law assigns a certain identity to individuals. This gives them distinct recognition. It also provides them with a sense of purpose. Obedience to the law empowers people to develop a unique definition of self-worth. However, the desire or intention to comply with the law is not intrinsically present. Most often, obedience mirrors the human need for conformism.

Conformity might allow individuals to shape their existence in the world according to their wishes. It implies obedience, and, in turn, identity. This identity, as I would argue, allows individuals to imbue their existence with meaning. However, it is important to acknowledge that identity has no correlation with anything innately present in humankind.

Nature and Society

Societies abound with many rules, but none are definitive. They may be bent, overlooked, or applied excessively, requiring strict enforcement. As the extent of enforcement can vary, so can the nature of that enforcement, based on factors detached from the rules themselves.

The enforcers of the law have the discretion to determine why, when, and how to enforce the rules. They often exercise an unparalleled level of control over these aspects. This control extends to the execution or location of enforcement. The significant responsibility placed on law enforcement personnel by this authority raises essential questions about accountability, fairness, and transparency in the administration of justice.

Inconsistency can arise from this subjectivity. Bias may affect the reinforcement or application of laws. It might lead to discriminatory practices. The aftermath of this reality could be vast and unpredictable, which may influence the criteria for rule implementation and determining the expected adherence to these rules.[14] Man-made rules fluctuate. They are unbound by their application or enforcement.

On the contrary, one might argue that natural laws are constant and unchanging. These laws are unalterable absolutes, thus negating the necessity of an obligation. Their manifestation is natural. Hence, there is no place for obligation within nature, as natural laws are non-negotiable. In a similar vein, the natural world does not require obedience, given its inherent constancy and lack of whimsicality.

---

[14] Let me point that I will not explore the issues from an ontological standpoint.

Chapter 3: Citizen Consent

What exists in nature is universal. It applies everywhere in the natural world. There are no exceptions to compliance. However, we cannot extend such a statement to manufactured laws. Every man perceives the world through a unique lens. Thus, men create laws as an arbitrary interpretation of the world around them.

Men, along with the world surrounding them, exist in a constant state of flux. Our understanding of ourselves and our world is constantly evolving. However, uncertainty about our identity, location, and trajectory prevails.

The laws function as anchors within this subjective reality. However, they themselves lack a clear identity. They have an erratic, elusive, and whimsical character. The transformation of these synthetic laws is not accidental. It is by design, I would contend. This process mirrors the ever-changing nature of society itself.

Although it is unnecessary to delve into the role of nature in the fabrication of laws, it is an important axiom of human jurisprudence. Manufactured laws often stand in contradiction to nature.

Natural laws, unlike human-created laws, do not intend to inflict punishment. Such synthetic laws inherently contradict the human spirit. Therefore, it becomes imperative to craft a convincing argument that challenges the notion of humans as inherently obedient.

Misclassification often miscalculates the concept of natural law. It is the law of the natural world. It is a concrete representation of the natural milieu itself.

It is common to conflate manufactured laws with natural laws. Yet, these fabricated laws, or positive laws, diverge from natural laws. The laws crafted by men are unequivocally artificial. As such, they cannot instill an inherent sense of obligation in one another. This characteristic is distinct, which also makes it noticeable. It stands in stark contrast to natural laws. One should never exchange these two concepts, especially in relation to citizen obligation.

Chapter 3: Citizen Consent

SECTION 2

FREE WILL & ULTIMATE TRUTH

CHAPTER 4

Theoretical Underpinnings of Obligation

When deliberating citizen obedience, two essential concepts arise. First, we engage with the idea of obedience, which has its roots in obligation. Here, obligation is a duty to act or refrain.

The previous perspective suggests an inherent proclivity among men to obey one another. It also suggests that there is a natural tendency of humans to follow rules established by others. This implies that obedience to the law is an intrinsic human desire. It proposes that the desire to obey the law is a fundamental aspect of human nature. However, I, in the present discourse, posit a counterargument.

The second concept relates to the notion of a citizenry. This term refers to the formation of a collective entity. It comes from a group and suggests a shared consciousness. This awareness occurs within a specific social context.

A prevalent idea suggests the independence of an individual from the collective. It positions the individual as an autonomous

Chapter 4: Theoretical Underpinnings of Obligation

entity. It suggests that an individual act or refrains from acting based on free will. Again, I would provide a differing viewpoint.

Examining the extent of obligation in men yields no uniform portrayal. The obligations of human civilization are not innate to man. Civilization is a construct of men, while a man is a product of nature.[1] Man's behavior within a civilized context does not mirror his natural state.

Obligation appears as an alien concept in man's natural understanding. Nature does not know of such a concept. It entails a propensity to act or abstain from acting. This perception of human nature shows that any imposed obligation is fundamentally unnatural. Hence, this requires induction, which is inescapable or devoid of permutability.

Obligation Theory

When discussing obligation theory, a prevalent belief suggests individuals have an inherent compulsion to adhere to the law.[2] Many esteemed scholars and observers propose that citizens hold a duty[3] or responsibility to comply with established laws, rules, or

---

[1] Please, keep in mind that I am not making a dogmatic argument in the present context.

[2] Most philosophers believe that everyone has a moral duty to obey the laws of his or her land. Nevertheless, the continuous debate in jurisprudence is between those who espouse a positivist approach to legal obligation and those who believe that nature is the source of obligation.

[3] In legal theory, people often use the term duty interchangeably with the term obligation.

orders within their respective jurisdictions.[4] Most often, notions of reason or morality predicate such views about legal obedience.

What then defines reason? The term implies an individual's ability to discern between just and unjust laws, to decide which to obey or disregard. Paradoxically, obedience often does not correlate with an individual's ability to reason.

Obedience lacks a discretionary aspect. The concept has no basis in reason. These two notions fundamentally contradict each other.

Each approach negates the other. However, society expects its members to obey all laws. Thus, in an ideal sense, no one is above the law. In the same way, ignorance does not justify legal violation.

Each law exists in expectation of obedience. Often, it is enforced rigorously. Noncompliance or nonenforcement can lead to giving up rights and privileges.

The presence of laws can foster a sense of freedom.[5] If a behavior is legally permissible, one might partake in it. On the contrary, laws can function as a tool to restrict social freedom. One might feel disinclined to behave in a certain manner if the authorities deem that behavior illegal.

Summarily, if an act is legal, one may be inclined to perform it. If it is illegal, one may refrain from it. This holds true regardless of the individual's needs or natural tendency to act or abstain.

---

[4] Leslie Green, "Legal Obligation and Authority," in *The Stanford Encyclopedia of Philosophy*, ed. Edward N. Zalta, Winter 2012 (Metaphysics Research Lab, Stanford University, 2012), https://plato.stanford.edu/archives/win2012/entries/legal-obligation/.

[5] Allan C. Hutchinson, *The Province of Jurisprudence Democratized*, 1 edition (Oxford ; New York: Oxford University Press, 2008).

Chapter 4: Theoretical Underpinnings of Obligation

A stringent legal system often treats the individual as an instrument, stripping them of self-determination. The individual becomes the property of the legal regime under which they live. This necessitates an obligation to obey the law, although individuals may perceive their duty differently. This is the danger inherent in the obligation.

Free Will

Obligation, by definition, curtails free will. Being simultaneously free and obligated presents a logical contradiction. Any assertion to the contrary would be a misinterpretation of the term self-determination.

Underpinning the concept of obligation is the principle that an individual governs their own reality. This subtly alludes to the idea of free will. It proposes that the individual dictates his circumstances. They have the power to shape their world within their constraints.

The implication is that an individual defines his existence within his world. This suggests that they are in control of their circumstances. As a result, they also choose their obligations. However, this assertion may not always be true. Obligation rarely presents as a choice. If people interlinked obligations and choice, no external constraints would bind them.

The concept of an obligation denotes the absence of choice. This lack of choice can lead to necessary action. However, it can also lead to abstention.

Free will implies a state of autonomy, independent of any influence, intrinsic or extraneous. However, a common belief is worthy of note in the present context. This belief posits that individuals are free out of necessity. The suggestion is that freedom becomes actualized only if it is desired.

This notion appears flawed and illogical. The indefensible worldview posits that these personal desires inherently predicate human actions. But is that really the case? This view lacks intellectual coherence under any circumstances.

Where then does this idea originate? What propels individuals to believe that their actions are based solely on their desires? Why should the world conform to the notions of right and wrong? Why should duality exist within beings? Is there a definitive truth within the world?

The Ultimate Truth

Free will and divinity create a clear ambivalence. The possession of one negates the possibility of the other. If one subscribes to a belief in a deity, personal freedom becomes untenable within the divine domain. If one upholds an ultimate truth, it follows that anything deviating from this absolute is false. Thus, free will and divinity cannot coexist.

It holds that a distortion of the truth equates to a falsehood, regardless of the extent of its skew. If it deviates from the absolute truth, then by definition, it is a lie. There is only one ultimate truth; any divergence is an untruth.

From a legal perspective, the concept of free will stands in stark contrast to the notion of citizen obedience. An [absolutely] free entity is bound by no laws or restrictions. On the contrary, individuals have obligations imposed on them by laws. Therefore, laws and freedom are mutually exclusive.

Laws, in their most benevolent state, restrict freedom. They confine entities within specific modes of existence. This

Chapter 4: Theoretical Underpinnings of Obligation

confinement dictates the parameters of their behaviors and their actions. Laws control behaviors. This control operates within defined environments. This eliminates any semblance of freedom.

Interestingly, conventional wisdom asserts that laws are essential to a free society. People view laws as the cornerstone of social structures. There lies a contradiction worth highlighting in this discourse.

In its ideal state, society is a platform that posits human emancipation from the grip of nature. It is supposed to eradicate primal instincts and bring about civility. Then, this ideal is also far from reality.

In truth, society becomes a confining space. It can be best described as mental confinement. But it is incapable of eradicating the inherent human nature.

People describe men by nature as beings of untamed disposition. Raw instincts have no limits. The purpose of the law seems paradoxical. It curbs man's innate tendencies. This is a complex concept to understand. This is an intriguing contradiction. It presents a unique paradox. A situation that is as confusing as it is interesting.

We consider laws to be restrictive measures. Nevertheless, laws do not suppress men's natural instincts. They are unable to curb the will of a person to ascend to civilization. Delving into the concept of unconditional obligation can help further understand this enigma.

The prevailing notion is that beings, inherently, are predisposed to abide by laws, whether grounded in nature or society. Some argue that this predisposition arises from the belief in a supreme truth that is only attainable by humans. Most observers believe that divine inspiration fuels this supreme truth.

We do not need to dissect the divine ordination of manufactured laws. We do not need to delve into human religious predispositions and dogmatic susceptibilities. Elsewhere, others have thoroughly examined these concepts. I, for instance, have explored this notion in the book titled *Natural Law: Morality and Obedience*.[6]

The idea of a single human-accessible truth is illogical. It represents an irrational worldview. This view is devoid of concrete evidence. It also lacks adaptable facts. This shows a conspicuous lack of intellectual breadth. However, it represents the human perspective. It underscores the seriousness with which humanity engages with life.

Human beings inherently seek knowledge. In our pursuit of the ultimate truth, we are relentless. We crave meaning. We seek understanding. Despite these efforts, we often fall short. At times, we must devise our own realities to confront reality itself. But invoking the existence of an absolute truth to justify our inability to comprehend our world is perilous.

Resorting to emotional arguments to rationalize the unknown or explicate the incomprehensible can be detrimental to humanity. Misconceptions about our world often fuel misunderstandings of reality itself. We need to address this issue. It reflects a narrow view.

A conduct code emanating from such a limited perspective could be harmful to the individual. I find it untenable to perceive the human world from this standpoint, nor can I accept legal principles defining human reality through such a prism. To me, it

---

[6] Refer to my publication, *Natural Law: Morality and Obedience*, to learn more about this understanding. Ben Wood Johnson, *Natural Law: Morality and Obedience* (Eduka Solutions, 2017).

is undeniable that manufactured laws and natural laws are inherently conflicting.

The core enforces the obligation to fabricate laws. Thus, it is never a choice; its obedience is never a voluntary act. Granted, you may disagree with this viewpoint. But before refuting it, allow me to further explain my stance. Allow me to provide clarity on the notion of a voluntary act.

CHAPTER 5

Obligation and God

The shared consensus in various literary circles contends that an entity superior to humans guides them in their worldly endeavors. We can identify this entity as "the truth." Then again, we must do so regardless of the nature of the truth itself or its form. People often refer to this entity as God or describe it as a divine spirit in various religious contexts.

Believers posit that the truth, or God, dwells within every individual. They argue that this presence reveals itself either through reason or adherence to divine commandments issued by a divine creator.[1] Yet, I would also argue that this simplistic reason cannot address obligation outside the scope of societal or cultural norms.

There is no inherent obligation in any social setting. However, society was built on consensus, which, in and of itself, induces all sorts of obligations, which, by any seeming, must be enforced and reinforced, sometimes under the threats of

---

[1] The term "creator" refers to the writings of the United States' declaration of independence, which states: "All men are created equal, that they are endowed by their creator with certain inalienable rights that among these are life, liberty, and the pursuit of happiness."

Chapter 5: Obligation and God

coercion. We could enforce the obligation or agree on this consensus.

A prevalent notion posits reason as the basis for social laws. I perceive these laws to be encapsulating the fury of the divine creator. Still, I find this perspective hard to reconcile.

Reason alone does not engender an inherent obligation to obey laws within a social setting. A person's capacity to reason does not predispose him to obedience. Reason does not function as a precursor to any sense of obligation.

The ability to reason does not connote any sense of duty in an individual. Such an assertion equates to perceiving the individual as a slave, either mental or physical. This is a viewpoint, which most would agree, is absurd.

Should one find themselves a slave, they would comprehend that their condition of confinement or state of subjugation is devoid of personal choice. Should one exist under the influence or authority of others, they would recognize the impossibility of relishing such a state of existence. Thus, the assertion that the capacity to reason compels an individual to behave in a certain manner is fallacious. Equally erroneous is the claim that reason obliges an individual to choose one course over another.

The ability to perceive the world through a rational lens empowers an individual to assert his unique identity therein. Possessing the capacity to reason would equip an individual with the means to interpret the world through an undistorted lens. He would interrogate the options presented to him.

If the individual cannot secure satisfactory explanations about the world or their role within it, they would seek alternate avenues to comprehend their reality in that milieu. He would strive to understand the alternatives presented to him; he would dismiss any course that does not resonate with his beliefs. That is, the individual could exercise genuine free will. But there is more to that argument.

An individual, having gained cognizance of his or her free will, would not seek to jeopardize it. The individual would strive to preserve his state of emancipation. They would renounce anything that might impede their free will. They would refrain from burdening themselves with any form of contract whether implied, explicit, social, or otherwise. Assuming otherwise would be myopic.

Obligation and Social Norms

The individual's capacity to reason is powerful. It may exert an influence over various aspects of his life. In this way, it shapes his existence. But it does so in certain manners and not in others. The individual, inherently aware of his natural state of being, might find that reason spawns conditional modes of obligation. Societal norms and values establish obligations. Without human intervention, their absence nullifies any sense of duty.

Obligations can arise out of compulsion. Such obligations can become irrefutable. Enforcement can be achieved through a variety of avenues. Some of these avenues include social customs and morals, among others.

I challenge the assertion that there is an inherent obligation to abide by the law. Society and the individual must imagine the conception of an obligation. My argument stands out, as it relies on the basis premise that laws, by their nature, do not have the power to instill inherent obligation.

The moral principles that give rise to laws also lead to obligations. A moral citizen would almost follow the law. On the contrary, an individual who does not subscribe to the moral

Chapter 5: Obligation and God

values of a society may show little inclination to adhere to its laws. Therefore, an obligation is relative to the degree to which a citizen recognizes the moral principles that resulted in the formation of a law. This recognition lends legitimacy to the existence of the obligation itself. Understanding this relationship between law and moral principles underscores the intricate interplay between individual beliefs, social norms, and legal constructs. It also highlights the importance of educating citizens about the underlying values that shape laws to foster a sense of shared responsibility and commitment to the rule of law.

In such a model, no legal obligation would exist only temporarily. This would reflect the law itself. The law is not a static; it is not an unchanging entity. Yet, this obligation would also be conditional. Provided that society adheres to its own rules, a majority would comply. Still, there will always be those who attempt to undermine these laws, potentially explaining the capricious nature of synthetic laws. To better understand this, let us consider the following perspective.

Should a society deviate from its most treasured values, obedience would lose its moral foundation. The laws may appear oppressive; it may provoke revulsion. This explains why autocratic rulers rarely endure in the long term. At some juncture, the populace would resist conformity.

Because of this understanding, one might argue that we must continuously enforce and fortify political or moral obligations. There is simply no way to bypass this necessity. What, then, does this imply about the obedience of citizens? Here is a plausible explanation.

Reinforcement of obligations cannot occur unless citizens perceive existing laws as fair. For instance, H. L. A. Hart refers to these as "fair laws" or "just laws." Then, these so-called just laws adopt the guise of social rules. These social rules stir up controversy when people view them as unfair or unjust. Let us examine a few hypothetical scenarios.

Renouncing Draconian Rules

The evolving nature of human laws is indisputable. Throughout history, social norms and legal statutes have undergone significant transformations. A bygone era may have been considered an act lawful, but current times may reject it. Similarly, in the past, certain conduct may have been accepted, but today may see it as unlawful.

Consider, for instance, the historic moment when many American states enforced laws preventing women from exercising their right to vote. People once regarded such laws as just. However, as society progressed, everyone universally recognized and acknowledged the injustice of these laws. This recognition was not a sudden revelation, but a gradual realization. Eventually, this led to their elimination. Most states had to eliminate such oppressive laws from their legislation.

There have been laws that support racism and various forms of discrimination. May people view the legislation that prevented African Americans from voting as unjust. Of course, such a law was likely to incite disobedience.

No one can contest the fact that laws possess fluidity. Legal status does not inherently imply morality, and, in turn, morality does not guarantee righteousness. An act that was once lawful can become unlawful, and a law contradicting the moral values of a certain epoch in society may not necessarily command obedience. This forms the crux of my argument.

Taking this into account, consider the following questions. How can obedience be inherent when it relies on transient moral values? When society persistently imposes obligations, how can an individual oblige himself in that milieu? How can reason induce obligation when obligation does not necessitate reason to obligate an individual? Obligation operates primarily on coercion, like brute force.

The Need of Obedience

The law almost demands adherence not necessarily to the specific statutes, but to the underlying idea of law itself. Disobedience always carries punitive consequences. These can range from monetary fines to incarceration. In extreme cases, they can even lead to capital punishment.

The laws enacted by humans are unrestricted in their enforcement, and their efficacy is primarily based on the extent of obedience they garner. Noncompliance with the spirit of the law often leads to drastic consequences.

There is no dispute that one must always obey the law. Each law carries an element of coercion. This makes obedience a condition. They do not treat it as a choice.

The expectation of obedience is not uniform for all social members. For example, those who enforce the law may enjoy exemptions from the very rules they uphold, rigorously at times. The same statute that charges law enforcers with maintaining may be violated by them.

Unlike those vested with discretion over law enforcement, the ordinary citizen is devoid of such privileges. The individual must adhere consistently to the law. A singular instance of non-compliance can expose the individual to the full might of the law.

Regardless of a person's record as a law-abiding citizen, a single transgression can have severe consequences. This prospect instills fear. It motivates individuals to adhere to the law. This adherence does not stem from the desire to be virtuous. Instead, it is primarily done out of fear of legal repercussions.

No one relishes being at odds with the law. Obedience, whether to the law or its enforcers, often arises from a desire to evade the punitive measures associated with legal transgressions. The law and its enforcement have the power to inspire fear in the populace.

Inspired by fear, most people opt to obey the law. Others will blindly comply with law enforcement directives. However, this compliance does not mean inherent righteousness.

In an ideal society that values objectivity, people would not perceive adherence to the law negatively. Law-abiding citizens would be beneficial both to society's order and to the integrity of the law. In such a setting, the enforcement might become redundant. This situation could lead to questions. But such questions would be about the necessity of laws. This presents a complex difficulty.

Under certain conditions, obedience would prove beneficial to most citizens. In an ideal exchange, one obeys the law and, in return, receives protection from law enforcers. However, reality often deviates from this ideal, with a stark difference between obeying the law and obeying law enforcers.

The previously mentioned distinction is subtle, but also significant. Obedience does not provide a guaranteed shield against the full extent of law enforcement authority. This still holds, even when laws are not infringed. This is what I refer to as the potent symbolism of law representation.

Chapter 5: Obligation and God

CHAPTER 6

Uncompromised Obedience

In pondering the concept of obedience, my focus does not lie on obedience towards the law. Although obedience is a necessary component of the idea of law, it is not the law itself. However, it is important to remember another aspect of legal or citizen obligation. The idea of law, in many cases, is the law itself both in its existence and its enforcement.

When contemplating the notion of law, one might propose that it could represent anything that diverges from the law, yet paradoxically symbolizes the law. For example, the police force is not the law in its legislative form. Nonetheless, it is always apt to perceive them as embodiments of the law.

The police operate as if they are the law themselves. Police officers behave themselves according to their discretion, sometimes violating the law, but imposing it when they consider it necessary. This notion extends to entire police departments or institutions.

Police institutions often wield power or authority. This power can be parallel to, or even surpass, the law they are appointed to uphold. The police often personify the law they enforce.

Chapter 6: Uncompromised Obedience

In many situations, the police stand as both the physical manifestation of the law and its symbolic representation. They anthropomorphize the laws, which they enforce arbitrarily at times. This dual role, being both enforcers and representatives of the law, places them in a position of elevated authority. This dilemma epitomizes the unique power wielded by the police.

Power

People often perceive power as a raw and coercive force that facilitates action. However, this term lacks a clear definition. Still, it is this same brute force that can force an individual or a collective to refrain from action. In its most basic form, we could perceive power as the ability to act. Alternatively, it could represent the freedom to refrain from acting facing no repercussions.

Power is the manifestation of a person's will or desire. In its most discernible embodiment, power can assume both tangible and ethereal forms. Its nature could be abstract, predicated on the notion of harm or the potential for it.

Authority often derives power from the legitimacy of the authority itself. If you were to think that you could harm me, I might perceive you as someone who could overpower me. I might even think that you have power over me. Similarly, if I were to admit that I could not resist or even counter your actions, you could effectively gain power over me. Power, in this context, is not static; it is ever-changing; it is fluid.

Granted, power is an intriguing concept. The reality of power can be misconstrued. However, power is inherently intricate and layered. Often, people perceive power as a force, which can actively enable a certain action; it may facilitate restraint. In any case, the profundity of power, in its most tangible sense, extends far beyond this rudimentary understanding.

Power, I would make the case, is the capacity to act or not to act. Conversely, power epitomizes the ability to abstain oneself or others from an action (or from acts) without facing adverse consequences. Power is the materialization of a person's will, wishes, or aspirations to be, to do, or to exist on their own and for their own sake. Power is intangible, though it can also be palpable in the most physical sense.

Power manifests itself in various forms. These forms can be both tangible and intangible. They traverse the physical and metaphorical realms. Its characteristics can sometimes be elusive and abstract, often hinting at the potential for harm or the perception of harm.

The complexity of power lies in its dual nature. Authority can be a source of security. It provides the ability to act. It also allows for the enforcement of wills. Simultaneously, authority can also be an instrument of oppression. This means that it can enable the imposition of will. It can also restrict others. This dual nature of authority requires careful consideration and balance in its application to ensure that it serves the interests of justice, fairness, and societal well-being.

The relationship between power and authority is important. Often, authority suggests power. An authority derives his (or its) capacity from a recognized or accepted position of influence. If you believe that you can harm me physically, emotionally, or otherwise, you may perceive yourself as having power over me. On the contrary, if I confess my inability to retaliate or protect myself against your actions, then people might perceive you as powerful compared to me.

The power dynamics are far from static. Such changing aspects can be manifested in a way that might not be fixed or

Chapter 6: Uncompromised Obedience

constant; instead, it is always fluid and ever-changing. The power potency changes and flows with changes in perception, circumstances, and context. As individuals or groups gain or lose influence, their power transforms accordingly. The dynamics of power are a continuum that reflects the complexities of human relationships and interactions.

Power, to reiterate, is not a zero-sum game. The notion reduces the concept of gaining power to doing so only at the expense of others. We can share power; it can grow; it can transform societies when harnessed effectively. However, power carries negative, if not irreversible, consequences. Thus, understanding the nature and dynamics of power is important in all aspects of human life, from politics and social structures to personal relationships and self-perception.

Power is a pervasive force that subtly shapes our actions, interactions, and our world. In the same way, there is a fine line between power an authority. One is guided by brutality; the other is based on a collective understanding, which affords those who yield it the legitimacy to exert it without fear of repercussions and in complete anonymity. Authority precedes power as power legitimizes authority and reinforces it.

Authority

We can understand authority as the capacity to perform an act. Alternatively, it can also mean the ability to not perform an act. The concept, in its tangible sense, stems from an underlying motive or necessity to act or abstain. An individual can either self-assign such authority or a group of people can confer it upon them.

The roots of authority often trace back to certain fundamental principles of behavior. Understandings about divinity or secularism may ground these principles. In most modern social contexts, the law affords authority. However, the holder of this authority simultaneously wields the power to act or to refrain from action. This sets the groundwork for the concept of a legal obligation.

The individual or the entity imbued with authority also possesses the power to impose obligations. With the power to obligate comes the authority to wield that power. This power can manifest itself as a raw, brute force or as a more subtle, gentle force.

Authority, in its essence, signifies the ability to perform or abstain from a particular act. It often originates from an underlying motivation, a fundamental necessity, or a situational imperative to act or to refrain the self from acting. This authority may be self-imposed. It comes from a person's own volition. Alternatively, a collective or a governing body can entrust it to an individual or a group of individuals.

Authority is deeply rooted in the foundational principles of conduct, which define and shape behavior norms. These principles are broad-based. They encompass the spectrum from divinity to secularism. This comprehensive approach forms the basis of these principles. They provide a moral or ethical framework that guides the exercise of authority, whether in the realm of religion, society, or state.

In the complex matrix of present-day social structures, the law is often the source of authority. Legal systems confer authority on certain individuals or entities. They trust them with the ability to act.

In addition, they give them the discretion to not act within defined parameters. This endowment of authority establishes the edifice of legal obligation. It places both constraints and responsibilities on those wielding power. This is an important aspect of the maintenance of legal and social order.

The authority given by law imbues individuals or entities with the power to impose obligations. This power is a significant corollary of authority. However, it is authority that legitimizes the exercise of power. It transforms power from a mere act of coercion. This transformation turns power into a sanctioned instrument of law. Yet, this transformative capacity for authority has profound implications for power.

The power that emerges from authority can manifest itself in a variety of ways. The range can extend from raw to unbridled force. It can also take a more nuanced and gentle form of influence. It can be explicit, visible in overt displays of authority, or it can be implicit, subtly woven into the fabric of social interactions and institutional practices. Regardless of its form, the exercise of power is an intrinsic aspect of authority. It shapes our understanding of legal obligations. It also forms our understanding of social norms.

Brute Force

A brute force represents the direct physical power used to force others. The police could epitomize this reality. The mere presence of the police instills obedience.

Such a presence signifies the tangible brute force that the police, as an institution, employ to enforce the law. Over time, this presence substantiates the utilization of force. This substantiation, in turn, elicits obedience.

The law can patent itself through the ramifications as a soft force. Potential punishment that may arise from law infringement can provoke obedience. The soft force, although it may not involve physicality, is a form of coercion.

The brute force embodies the application of direct physical might, an unfiltered exercise of power that commands compliance. An emblematic example of this is the police force. The sheer presence of police officers in public spaces often serves to elicit obedience among citizens. This signifies an immediate physical manifestation of the law's authority. When citizens see police officers, they remember the law and its power.

The police force exemplifies the palpable raw exertion of power used by the institution to enforce the law and maintain social order. Physical presence manifests this power in its most unequivocal manner. Immediate actions also exhibit this. Such power exerts a pervasive influence on citizen behavior, which in turn facilitates an atmosphere of order and obedience. As time passes, this persistent visibility becomes more evident. The application of brute force becomes more prevalent. Both factors merge its efficacy. This, in turn, prompts compliance and deterrence among the population.

Soft Force

Unlike brute force, soft force is much more malleable. This type of manifestation of power in the most physical sense also encapsulates the intangible repercussions of the law. It manifests itself not through physical presence or action, but through the looming threat of potential punishment arising from a violation of legal norms. This punishment, though not necessarily immediate or tangible, is not continually permanent. However, it casts a pervasive shadow of consequence that stimulates obedience.

Chapter 6: Uncompromised Obedience

The soft force, although lacking a physical dimension, represents a distinct form of coercion. The implicit threat of legal penalties, ranging from fines to imprisonment, underscores the authority of the law. It stresses the authority's capacity to impose consequences for noncompliance.

Soft force is an important aspect of legal obligation. Thus, it incites the obedience of the citizen in the most tangible sense. This form of power, while subtle, is nonetheless a compelling motivator of obedience. It underscores the multifaceted nature of legal authority. It outlines the various mechanisms it employs to enforce compliance.

CHAPTER 7

Power of the Law

In a void of law, any individual possesses both the authority and the power to act or refrain from action. However, a law coming into play strips that individual of personal authority. The commanding power of the law replaces the individual's sense of free will.

The dynamics of power in society are complex. The concept can encompass physical power, mental power, intellectual power, sectarian power, majority power, and instrumental power. Each of these forms of power would induce a sense of fear. They would also be enough to instill a propensity for obedience in anyone. This would be the case even if these forms of power were standing alone or on their own.

In a landscape devoid of laws, an individual inherently holds both the authority and the power to determine his actions, free from external influences. The realm of choice in such scenarios is boundless; individuals navigate their lives according to their free will and personal judgment. They are unencumbered by any societal norms or codified rules. However, introducing the law led to a tectonic shift in this dynamic.

Chapter 7: Power of the Law

The advent of the law strips individuals of their personal authority. Their behavior is directly influenced by the system of codified norms and regulations imposed on them by the law, which serves as an authoritative framework. The individual's sense of free will, once untamed and unbounded, is now under the jurisdiction of the law. The law asserts its commanding power. It supersedes personal freedom to act or abstain from action. It demands adherence. It shapes behavior under its edicts.

The labyrinth of power dynamics within a society is intricate and multifaceted. Power manifests itself in numerous forms, each with distinct characteristics and implications. Physical power harnesses brute strength. Mental power leverages psychological influence.

Intellectual power capitalizes on knowledge and cognitive competence. Sectarian power derives its strength from religious or ethnic affiliations. Most of the power exploits the strength of numbers. Instrumental power utilizes resources and tools as levers of influence. Understanding these various forms of power provides a nuanced view of how influence operates within different contexts and relationships. It lays the groundwork for analyzing the dynamics of control, collaboration, including in conflict in social, political, and economic systems.

Each of these forms of power, individually, has the capacity to instill a sense of apprehension or prompt obedience within those on the receiving end of its exertion. They serve as invisible threads pulling on the marionettes of social order. This force compels individuals to act in certain ways.

Expectations, norms, or direct commands push them to comply. These facets of power, whether discreetly woven into the fabric of everyday life or explicitly wielded, paint a nuanced portrait of how authority shapes societal behavior and individual decision-making.

Legal Power

As we progress in this dialogue, we must consider the concept of legal power which is rooted in the law itself. This form of power can manifest itself in numerous ways. People often perceive its expression as a tool used to enforce authority. In fact, the tool is the power itself.

One could argue that power gives a tangible form to the concept of law. This manifestation of power that upholds and enforces the law is what I term the "Rule of Law" in the present context. Permit me to delve further into this concept.

Delving into the intricacies of legal power requires an understanding of its origin. The legal power germinates from the fertile ground of the law. This unique form of power transcends the simple authority of an individual or institution. It is, rather, the collective embodiment of shared norms and values of a society crystallized within the framework of the law. The populace collectively accepts, invigorating it.

This manifestation of power is distinctive; it is the expressed authority derived from the legitimacy of the law. Often, people consider legal power as a critical tool. They use it as a conduit to enforce the authority that the law vests in them. However, this conceptualization barely scratches the surface. Beyond being a mere tool, power is the quintessential substance of the law; the raw, vibrant energy that allows the existence, potency, and efficacy of the law.

One might argue that it is a power that breathes life into the abstract notion of law. Legal systems are underpinned by the scaffolding of the law itself. It gives form to the law's mandates. It also provides structure and effect. The Rule of Law, as I call it, is this tangible manifestation of power? It is not merely an abstract principle or a philosophical ideal, but a palpable force that upholds and enforces the tenets of law.

The rule of law embodies the fair and equitable enforcement of laws. It ensures that everyone is subject to the law's authority. This happens regardless of a person's current social status or personal connections. It advocates the tenets of justice, fairness, and accountability, which are fundamental to any well-functioning society.

The rule of law does not simply refer to the blind enforcement of statutes. It encompasses the creation of an environment characterized by transparency, predictability, and certainty, allowing individuals to exercise their rights, fulfill their responsibilities, and seek redress for complaints. At the core of a democratic society lies this concept. It reinforces the idea that no one is above the law.

The rule of law, I would contend, is more than a mere enforcement mechanism. It is the living embodiment of shared values and collective aspirations of a society, expressed through the lens of law. As we further dissect this concept, we see that the rule of law is an agent of power. It is also an artifact of power. This duality reflects the intricate relationship between power, authority, and law in society. Understanding this relationship provides insight into the mechanisms that govern social order and the ways in which legal principles interact with human behavior and cultural norms.

Rule of Law

It is important to understand the dynamics between citizens, law enforcement, and the laws they enforce. The dynamics of power and how these realities play out in practice are more potent than the abstract understanding of the law itself.

The authority given to law enforcement agencies and officers becomes the primary driver of compliance or obedience. These individuals and entities have been assigned the responsibility of law enforcement. In this context, the emphasis is on their role and authority, not on the law itself. This perspective raises questions about the balance between authority and the intrinsic value of the law. They raise question about how these factors influence public perception and adherence to legal norms.

This dynamic suggests that actual laws may become secondary to the power exercised by those entrusted with their enforcement. As such, the interaction of the citizens with these enforcement agencies becomes the primary avenue of their experience with the law. This interaction often takes the form of commands or directives issued by law enforcement officers. Understanding this dynamic may help frame the importance of trust, transparency, and professionalism within law enforcement agencies. It highlights the need for continuous dialogue, education, and collaboration between the public and law enforcement to foster a legal system that reflects the principles of justice and equality. One could argue that, in such situations, citizens are expected and forced to obey the laws, not the law itself.

This implies that law enforcement officers often expect citizens to follow directions even when they have not violated any law. Perceiving and treating any failure to comply with these directives as disobedience. This perception can have potential legal consequences. This reality raises ethical issues and highlights the need for clear guidelines, accountability, and public awareness of the rights and responsibilities of law enforcement officers and citizens. It stresses the importance of a legal system that prioritizes fairness, respect for individual rights, and trust between law enforcement and the community.

This reality also raises questions about the balance of power, the rights of citizens, the role of law enforcement, and the nature of obedience and compliance. Should we restrict the power of law enforcement to protect the rights of citizens? Are there scenarios in which citizens should have the right to resist or not comply with law enforcement directives, especially when they are not violating any law? How can citizens and law enforcement establish a more equitable power dynamic?

These are complex issues that touch on legal philosophy, human rights, social norms, and ethical considerations. Society, policymakers, and legal scholars will continue to grapple with these questions. They must do so to ensure a balance between the duty of law enforcement to maintain order and the rights of citizens.

In a further detailed examination of the concept of "rule of law,' we find a concept of remarkable complexity and profound influence. The rule of law does not represent an impersonal, mechanical application of statutes and regulations. Society, power dynamics, and human behavior deeply embed it instead. Therefore, understanding this rule requires more than just a rudimentary grasp of legal texts; it requires a comprehension of the interplay between individuals, institutions, and their surrounding social context.

It is important to aptly highlight a key part of the rule of law; that is, the role of law enforcement agencies in the law itself and/or its applications. In fact, these agencies and their officers are the human face of the law, the physical embodiment of its directives. Thus, they receive substantial power and authority. This ensures the effective administration and enforcement of the laws.

The underlying forces between law enforcement and the citizenry are far from simple. The authority conferred upon law enforcement is not merely a tool of compulsion but a mechanism that engenders compliance or obedience. Therefore, coercion does not characterize only the interaction between citizens and law enforcement; it is a complex dance where power, respect and a shared understanding of societal values play important roles.

This dynamic between the law and its enforcement raises concerns about the potential for power misuse. When the application of law enforcement authority becomes the primary driver of obedience, there is a risk that it overshadows the law itself. The law, in its true essence, could risk becoming secondary to the authority exercised by its enforcers. This disjuncture can create an imbalance. Fear or coercion, rather than respect for the law and shared societal values, drives obedience, nothing else does.

The term "rule of law" hinges on the careful balance between enforcement and the principles embodied by the law. It demands a delicate equilibrium between the power of law enforcement and the rights and liberties of the citizenry. This balance is of utmost importance.

Democratic societies consider it the cornerstone. It ensures that the law is followed. It guarantees an equitable application of these laws. This approach fosters respect for the dignity of every individual. It does so by promoting the values of equality and fairness. In doing so, it nurtures a just and harmonious society.

The concept of rule of law refers to the enforcement of legal norms. However, it is also about maintaining the fine line between authority and individual liberties. It is a continuous process of negotiation and readjustment, of balancing the need for order with respect to individual rights and the principles of justice.

As we further delve into these dynamics, we must also recognize that the rule of law is a living and breathing concept. It does not remain static but rather changes with time. This continuous evolution mirrors that of society and its norms. Society continually strives to uphold not just a principle, but also to fulfill a commitment to justice, fairness, and equity.

CHAPTER 8

Authority of Law Enforcement Officers

When it comes to the authority of law enforcers, it is important to consider some of the controversial aspects of law enforcement practices. One such practice is the "Stop and Frisk" program, which has led to a significant debate. The discussion focuses on the power dynamics between citizens and law enforcement. It highlights concerns about the rights of individuals against arbitrary and potentially discriminatory practices by the police and other law enforcement entities. These issues underscore the importance of scrutiny, regulation, and community involvement in shaping law enforcement policies that respect individual rights and build trust within society.

Critics have attacked the "Stop and Frisk" policy for possible racial profiling. They also highlight potential violations of civil rights and erosion of public trust in law enforcement. Critics argue that these types of policy give law enforcement too much discretionary power. The understanding is that someone can easily misuse this power. As a result, discriminatory practices and the violation of individual rights can occur.

Chapter 8: *Authority of Law Enforcement Officers*

The assertion of power by law enforcement, especially in encounters with citizens, can also escalate situations unnecessarily. This reality can lead to negative consequences. Law enforcement must find a balance between asserting their authority to maintain order and individuals asserting their rights.[1]

Finding this balance is important, as it can help maintain public trust in law enforcement, which is essential for law enforcement to perform their duties. It is a complex issue. Thus, it requires careful consideration and dialogue between lawmakers, law enforcement agencies, and communities.

A citizen interacting with a law enforcement officer in contentious circumstances makes up a delicate situation. The perception of authority, the dynamics of power, and the potential for escalation contribute to this delicate balance. It is important that society engages in dialogues on these topics. There is a need to ensure the rights and safety of all citizens. There is a need to maintain the integrity of law enforcement agencies.

Law Enforcement Practices

The *stop and frisk* policy outlined earlier, along with similar approaches, provokes contention in society. This is because they might exacerbate the power dynamics between law enforcers and citizens. It brings to sharp relief the tension between ensuring public safety and preserving individual rights against undue and prejudiced interventions.

The *stop and frisk* policy has been at the forefront of discourses on racial profiling, civil rights violations, and the

---

[1] This law was mostly prevalent in the State of New York. There, police officers have the right to stop any citizen for whatever the reason.

diminishing trust in law enforcement. Critics argue that such policies accord an excess of discretionary power to law enforcement. Power is also a topic of contention. Critics argue that power is always ready for misuse by law enforcement entities. They are concerned that this could lead to discriminatory practices and infringement of individual rights.

This discretionary power given to law enforcers under such policies rises probing questions about authority in law enforcement. It forces us to grapple with the nebulous boundary between maintaining law and order and potentially infringing on individual rights and freedoms. What amount of power should we grant to law enforcers? Where should we draw the line to prevent this power from being exploited?

The issues of discriminatory practices and civil rights violations tied to the *stop and frisk* policy underscore a critical point about the authority of law enforcers. They must not exercise their authority unbridled. Instead, they must bind them by the strict principles of fairness, justice, and respect. They should treat all individuals fairly, regardless of their race, ethnicity, or socioeconomic status.

The erosion of public trust in law enforcement is a critical concern. The legitimacy of law enforcers depends heavily on public trust. Trust inevitably becomes compromised when the balance of power tips towards excessive authority and away from citizen rights. Therefore, to serve and protect law enforcement, it must balance its authority with a profound respect for the rights of citizens, thus fostering public trust and cooperation.

The controversy surrounding the *stop and frisk* policy serves as a powerful reminder of the need for continued oversight, transparency, and accountability in law enforcement. It highlights the importance of upholding the principles of fairness and justice, not just in the law's letter, but also in its enforcement. It compels

Chapter 8: *Authority of Law Enforcement Officers*

us to strive for equilibrium. Yet, this equilibrium is one in which the authority of law enforcers and the rights of citizens are harmoniously balanced. This balance facilitates a climate of mutual respect and trust.

Forced to Obey

In every circumstance, compliance with societal regulations remains a non-negotiable obligation of the citizen. A person must never disobey the law. Failure to fulfill this commitment can lead to a multitude of unintended consequences.

Consider Garry's case, an African American individual. He was late for work. This situation led to a rash decision on his part. He ignored the traffic signal. In the aftermath, a police officer intercepted him. Understanding that he had violated the law, Garry was ready to accept the resulting repercussions of his actions.

As the officer approached Gary, the young man observed a drastic change in his tone. The officer's hand was menacingly placed on his weapon. This suggested that the officer perceived Gary as a potential threat. The officer's hostility was apparent to Garry, as the officer's action silently communicated an intent to harm the young man.

Law enforcement officials tend to view the offender through a different lens. Empowerment may arise within the officer. This often allows him to engage condescendingly with the citizens. Their interaction changes the power dynamics. Racial and discriminatory practices or racial profiling might intensify this behavior. The previous encounters of the citizen with the law, whether they have a criminal history or preceding transgressions, do not matter in this situation.

In the realm of law, obedience is a constant expectation, a requirement. No one, as the theory goes, should be above the law. Yet, specific groups seldom realize this ideal. In fact, most people are above the law, especially when the violator of the said law is a person or s group of individuals in position of power.

Obedience, in a legal context, presents itself capriciously. A dual standard characterizes this obedience. Recall that law enforcement agencies often operate as if they are on top of the law. However, the blame cannot be put on their shoulders. It is the construction of the law that inherently invites such behavior.

Societal norms, established practices, and the nature of law enforcement duties can sometimes create a perception among officers. This perception leads them to believe that they have an elevated status above the ordinary citizen. This belief can have serious implications for the relationship between law enforcement and the public. It may affect interactions, trust, and overall effectiveness of law enforcement in maintaining public safety while respecting the rights and dignity of individuals. This might lead to misinterpretation of situations, abuse of power, and unequal enforcement of the law.

Garry, an African American man, exemplifies some of the serious issues that can arise in law enforcement interactions when a police officer stops him. Implicit bias, stereotyping, and racial profiling can distort the perception of situations. This may cause unfair treatment. Many people recognize and criticize this problem.

All citizens must obey the law; such an expectation is always irrefutable. However, it is important to note that law enforcement officers, while granted certain powers to uphold the law, are also subject to the law, at least in theory. They must adhere to established guidelines. They must follow protocols and laws.

These rules protect the rights of individuals and prevent the misuse of power.

The challenges in translating this theory into practice are significant. It is important that we continue to promote and uphold the principles of justice, fairness, and equality in the law's enforcement. This includes making sure that we treat all citizens with dignity and respect, regardless of their racial or ethnic background. It also includes not tolerating any form of discrimination.

At the same time, it is important to recognize the difficult and sometimes dangerous situations that law enforcement officers face. However, a person must judge their actions within the context of these situations. Yet, there is a need to hold them accountable for any abuses of power.

The issues echoed in this dialogue so far are fundamental to the ongoing discussions of law enforcement practices, civil rights, and social justice. There is an urgent need for these conversations to lead to actionable reforms. We must ensure that we uphold the rule of law fairly for all citizens.

The Imperative of Compliance

The imperative of complying with social regulations underscores an unavoidable fact of citizenship. We not only expect but also demand steadfast adherence to the law. It is through this submission that a society must operate under some semblance of order. However, failure to fulfill this commitment can precipitate a cascade of unintended consequences that extend beyond the immediate transgression.

The case of Garry illustrates the delicate balance between individual judgment and adherence to the law. It reveals how context and personal circumstances can influence decision-making in everyday situations. It also serves as a reminder of the ubiquitousness of legal norms and their role in shaping behavior and social expectations when it comes to obligation.

Garry's story extends beyond a personal case of rule breaking. The illustration shows the inevitability of law enforcement. It also shows to what extent individuals are expected to obey social norms and regulations. The automatic assumption that Garry must face repercussions for his actions highlights a vital aspect of our legal system. However, it is undeniable that the enforcement of laws is based on the threat of consequences. This threat encourages obedience.

The mere fact that threats must induce obedience reveals an underlying principle. Legal compliance requires this compliance. Often, fear of punishment rather than an intrinsic believe in the law's righteousness motivates obedience in this case. Such a system invites questions about the moral foundation of legal norms and the role of education, culture, and community participation in fostering a deeper understanding and acceptance of the rule of law.

It is also important to note that the legal obligation to obey does not simply stem from a fear of sanctions. A social contract, inherent and understood, underpins society. Presumably, citizens implicitly agree to this when they participate in society. This agreement is rooted in a collective understanding that obedience to the law, irrespective of its apparent insignificance or immediate inconvenience, is vital to maintaining social order.

When we examine Garry's experience, we must consider the tension between personal convenience and societal obligation. The law reminds us that we must obey it not by choice but by requirements. Potential penalties and societal expectations reinforce this requirement. The bedrock upon which our society is built underscores our commitment to the rule of law, which is guided by our expectations to obey the law, a reality that undermines any notion of inherent predisposition for obedience.

CHAPTER 9

The Nature of Fabricated Laws

The fabric of any law is subjective. It is whimsical. A variety of factors influence its inception and enforcement. The creation of laws lacks an objective basis; it is inherently subjective.

Every law aims to govern a particular group of people. Its enforcement is assigned to a specific group. Its impact as well as its applications are unilateral.

These synthetic laws present an intriguing aspect; you cannot implement them from a standpoint of neutrality. Someone must first break the law before enforcing it. This paradox, which I refer to as the precocity of fabricated laws, adds to the complexity of law enforcement.

The violator of the law can vary; sometimes, it is the ordinary citizen; at other times, the enforcer themselves. Sometimes, it can be both. However, there is discernible selectivity in the execution or enforcement of legal rights. In such cases, obedience requires coercion.

Imagine a scenario. In this situation, Albert was on the highway. He was speeding and exceeding the limit by twenty miles. A state trooper had tried to pull him over. However, to intercept Albert, the trooper had to exceed Albert's speed, breaking the same law that he was intending to enforce.

This situation raises a fundamental question. Why should Albert comply with the trooper when both violated the law? There is no one-size-fits-all answer to this dilemma. This predicament, the one of law enforcement and citizen obedience, is what I term the law enforcement-citizen obedience dilemma.

A Paradox of Laws

At the heart of any legal system, we find a paradox. That is, laws, though designed as a bastion of objectivity and fairness, are inherently subjective in their formulation. This capriciousness arises from a myriad of influences that shape the inception and enforcement of any statute. Laws, being the creations of human thought, are whimsical and changeable. They are based not on a singular objective reality, but on a confluence of subjective perceptions, intentions, and necessities.

The design of each statute, decree, or regulation has the aim of governing a certain group. It regulates a particular aspect of human life. These laws cater to specific scenarios and contexts, inevitably leaving the impression of the bias of a unilateral application. Therefore, all members of a society seldom experience its impact evenly. This raises questions about the fairness and impartiality of such laws.

Adding further to this layered complexity is the unique puzzle that I call the "precocity of fabricated laws." This approach posits that to enforce a law, there needs to be a violation of it first. The law then remains in limbo until someone transgresses it. Thus, the law only gains tangible form through its infringement. It takes action to rectify the violation. The goal is to restore order.

This inherent precocity presents an intriguing ambivalence. That is, the enforcement of laws occurs reactively. However, its mere existence serves as a proactive deterrent to unlawful behavior. This contradictory nature of laws, their existence contingent on violation, yet thriving on compliance, lays bare the conundrum of law enforcement.

There is a need to reconsider our assumptions about the inherent fairness and impartiality of the law to understand the capricious nature of fabricated laws. Instead, we find a system shaped by human subjectivity. It is a malleable framework subject to interpretation, enforcement, and the continual influence of societal evolution.

Selective Obedience

In the United States, legislators and law enforcement officials often operate on the edges of legality. Sometimes, they even act as though they exist above the law. The legislators have the capacity to circumvent the law. They often do so by constructing legal frameworks that provide them immunity from the laws they have enacted.

Those who devise the laws have the power to also draft laws that function as protective barriers against other laws. Such laws shield them from the ramifications of laws they have previously implemented. It is neither a stretch of the truth nor intellectually dishonest to suggest that law enforcement often exercises discretion in which laws to enforce and under what circumstances.

Chapter 9: The Nature of Fabricated Laws

In this context, it can hardly be said that society's members intrinsically have the obligation to comply with the law. In fact, the law or its enforcers sometimes force some individuals to relinquish their will, whether free or otherwise. However, people seldom voluntarily surrender such a will; typically, raw power or its threat enforces it.

The compliance with the law is a coercive principle. If left unsupervised, most people would ignore the law. But a political obligation to respect the law is always present.

Laws function as tools of limitation and instruments of constraint. But this contradicts fundamental human instincts. Even so, only a handful of people would dare defy the authority of a legitimate entity aiming to regulate their behavior. Consequently, at its core, every obligation is inherently political.

The sense of moral duty is intimately linked to political obligation. A citizen might believe that they control their obligations under or under the law. However, established norms and values usually predetermine their choices. Citizens may find themselves with no choice but to abandon any semblance of free will they once possessed.

The role of morality in legal obedience is a topic worth exploring. A commonly held belief posits morality as the basis for the intellectual argument supporting societal legal obligation. As highlighted in the present context, this perspective is flawed.

Distinguishing between natural law and positive law is a challenging task, particularly in practical terms. There is no clear-cut compass to differentiate the two concepts. The domains of morality and obligation suffer from a lack of a sound intellectual justification for laws. Misconceptions ground a legal obligation.

The arguments I have laid out here so far suggest that our understanding of natural law is incomplete. We misinterpret the nature of positive law. Neither approach provides a firm foundation for elucidating nor contextualizing legal obedience within society.

A Complex Democratic Politics

America is a vibrant and complex democratic state. However, it is not immune to the vagaries of selective obedience to the law, especially amongst its policymakers and law enforcement agencies. This phenomenon, while not exclusive to any one society or political system, carries a unique flavor within the realm of the American sociopolitical landscape.

Lawmakers, by virtue of their positions, wield considerable influence over the legal framework of the state. This authority often extends beyond the mere drafting and enactment of laws. It spills into an arena where those in power can engineer legal constructs. These paradigms effectively insulate them from the regulations they codify. This practice raises concerns about accountability, transparency, and ethical use of power within the legal system. It underscores the need for mechanisms that ensure the equitable application of laws and prevent abuse of authority for personal or political gain. Thus, those who craft laws can deftly sidestep the repercussions of their legislative products while remaining within the confines of legal propriety.

Creating laws that function as protective barriers against other laws is a strategic maneuver that provides some immunity to lawmakers. It is an architectural feat of legislative drafting that reveals an unsettling truth about the interplay of power and law. These self-serving constructs can protect legislators. They protect them from the effects of the laws they have previously ratified. This situation generates a peculiar form of selective legal obedience. But that is not all.

Chapter 9: The Nature of Fabricated Laws

Law enforcement agencies also participate in the practice of selective obedience. Charged with the duty to uphold the law, these entities frequently find themselves in positions where discretion becomes necessary. The choice of which laws to enforce, when to enforce them, and under what circumstances is often subject to a myriad of influences, both internal and external. It is thus not an overreach to observe that law enforcement can (and does) exercise discretion in its application of the law.

Such selective obedience presents us with an intricate web of issues and dilemmas. Challenge our understanding of the concepts of legal obligation, fairness, and justice. It forces us to reckon with the complexities of a system in which those who plan and enforce the laws possess the means to navigate their ramifications selectively.

SECTION 3

ASSESSING THE NATURE OF REASON

CHAPTER 10

The Notion of Reason

We can divide the notion of reason into two distinct categories: natural reason and social reason. Here, natural reason relates to an inherent, innate logical sense. Social reason represents a utilitarian form of reasoning. It emerges within and adapts to social contexts. However, natural reason is not a universal concept. It does not limit the capacity of human beings to reason within specific domains.

Social reasons have a more restricted view. Within social dynamics, the faculty of reason is synonymous with the ability to discern right from wrong. This is a fundamentally utilitarian approach to human reasoning. While this viewpoint is valid, it is also arguable that the concept of reason extends beyond the merely deciphering of ethical correctness.

Societal contexts derive the notion of reason from moral constructs. It is a by-product of natural law theories. But "Reason" is often used to signify ideas of justice, rationality, and appropriateness. We often use the foundational principles of reason to delineate the degree of alignment with moral standards.[1]

The prevailing societal belief posits that every human being inherently has the capability to reason. Echoing Thomas Aquinas's sentiments, we consider humans as "reasonable creatures"[2] from inception. They are capable (and expected) to reason within societal confines.

People presume that reason will always guide an individual to discern between right and wrong. Intuitively, we believe that humans lean towards justice rather than evil. However, if this premise were true, it would also raise the question of why laws, as societal norms governing behavior, exist in the first place.

Refuting the Concept of Reason

If reason were to be the fundamental driving force behind legal obedience, it would imply a specific assumption. This assumption is that every individual has the capacity for reason. Following this logic, reason itself should instill a sense of obligation within the individual.

The idea that only rationality might motivate obedience to the law sparks a complex discussion of human nature. It also raises the topics of ethics and the relationship between individual conscience and social norms. In this hypothetical context, the individual would almost elect good over evil. This would effectively eliminate the need for an enforced obligation.

---

[1] Brian H. Bix, *Jurisprudence: Theory and Context*, Fifth edition (Durham, N.C: Carolina Academic Press, 2009).

[2] Ibid., 73.

The notion of obligation would become inherent, self-imposed, and self-regulated if such a concept was needed. However, it is evident that this conceptualization of reason borders on the fantastic. This paradox underscores my principal argument, which echoes that the current understanding of reason appears incongruent.

In the sphere of lived experiences, reason does not function in such a linear manner. Note that I do not contend that humans lack the ability to reason. Granted, my argument is more nuanced.

Every individual navigates their world through a unique lens. The person subsequently uses reason in divergent ways. The notion of a universalized approach to human reasoning becomes untenable and unnecessary.

Reason can only attain universal status if someone imposes or indoctrinates it. Moral teachings infuse numerous paradigms of reason. When we reach a consensus on a particular course of action, reason assumes a universal guise. This also applies to an accepted mode of behavior. Consensus occurs regardless of the wisdom or moral integrity of such actions.

This observation leads to a reflection on how social agreement can sometimes overshadow critical thinking and ethical considerations. It also prompts us to examine more closely the formation of collective norms. It echoes the role of education in the promotion of rational discourse. At the same time, it reveals the need for vigilance against the potential erosion of individual judgment and moral responsibility.

This argument does not imply that certain individuals cannot reason beyond societal boundaries. It remains essential to highlight the intricate nature of reason. The concept of reason is not a homogeneous construct. Rather, it is a variable personal attribute.

There is an accepted "universal standard" for reasoning.[3] However, the extent of its universality rests on collective agreement. Thus, the universally accepted standard is not necessarily universal in its truest form. Instead, it is a consensus-agreed method for evaluating human reasoning. There is a need to delve further into the multifaceted concept of reason.

Types of Reasons

There are distinct types of reasoning, each with a potentially different universal understanding. Take, for instance, Budziszewski's concept of "Practical Reason." This concept suggests that we can understand reason as an aspect of prudence.[4] Budziszewski states: "Prudence is our capacity to reach choices on the basis of deliberation because practical reason deals with contingent truths; it is concerned with things that can be other than they are."[5]

This reference suggests that reason can be rooted in individual perception. This approach also aligns with my contention of "multiplicity" in reasoning. An exploration into the function of reason in legal obligation thus becomes a pertinent aspect of this discourse.

Obligation necessitates coercion, a process potentially stripping individuals of their free will, if it existed at all. The notion of purity is antithetical to that of obligation; for pure reason, this would incite the individual to resist any obligation.

---

[3] I am referring to the notion of "a reasonable person test."

[4] J. Budziszewski, *Written on the Heart: The Case for Natural Law* (Downers Grove, Ill: IVP Academic, 1997).

[5] Ibid., 59.

Not everyone understands the concept of reason in the same way. Therefore, it is not a universal connotation that underscores a particular understanding. The proposition that the principles of reason form the foundation for the obligation suggests that reason could induce conformity. A universally accepted interpretation of reason would give rise to collective conformity, general compliance, and legal obedience.

The reason behind compliance with the law may not reflect the perspectives of others. The sense of obligation of one person can vary from that of another. This introduces a level of subjectivity. This subjectivity further complicates the formulation of a sound argument. In this case, people may have an inherent sense of justice and injustice and understand how to act or refrain from acting under certain circumstances. The political obligation to the law remains paramount.

The law might invalidate an individual's sense of obligation toward their actions or lack thereof. The law prescribes a certain course of action. Non-compliance can have undesirable consequences. Sometimes, the law may force an individual to abandon his judgment and conform.

Pure reason might instill a sense of obligation in the individual. However, this obligation would not be rooted in coercion. The individual could decide to obey the law based on a calculated assessment of personal benefits.

Others in society might perceive their obligation differently. This perception can vary widely from person to person. This difference in perception often leads to a lack of cohesion. Obligation might not produce uniformity, which might affect conformity within the social environment. Individual actions may not align with the views of other members of society.

If we consider reason to be unrestricted or unconstrained, society will only suffer a trivial difference from the wilderness.

Chapter 10: The Notion of Reason

Reason, as humans understand it, is a defining trait of our species. One could argue that humans do not hold the exclusive ability to reason.[6] However, such an argument is reserved for another discourse or another literary journey.

Regulating Conducts

Human beings are the only species that have laws that regulate their behavior. This reality suggests that we either view ourselves as unreasonable or that we are indeed. Perceiving humans as unreasonable would also account for the necessity of laws to establish a semblance of universality and justify compliance or conformity. The laws instill reason in human beings. Thus, the argument lacks intellectual weight if it states that humans, as reasonable beings, must adhere to the law. If that were to be the case, laws would be unnecessary since humans, as rational entities, would almost act righteously. The assumption here is that everyone would behave appropriately.

The existence of laws that enforce a universal mode of conduct suggests that humans perceive themselves as unreasonable. It also suggests that humans acknowledge the absence of free will. Implementing laws promotes cohesion among members of the species.

Laws are fundamentally coercive; hence, they cannot give freedom. To put it simply, telling a child, "I know you know what to do, but I must ensure that you do what you must" involves multiple implications. It suggests a lack of trust in the child to act

---

[6] Refer to my publication about the subject (Cogito, Ergo Philosophus). This work examines the notion of reason and human thinking. Ben Wood Johnson, *Cogito, Ergo Philosophus: I Think, Therefore I Philosophize* (Tesko Publishing, 2019).

correctly. This statement reflects a wider theme in the dynamics of authority and obedience. It highlights the tension between control and trust.

It reveals the development of personal responsibility. It may also shed light on the way in which societal norms mirror these interpersonal interactions. Legal structures also reflect these interactions. Both elements play a role in shaping the behavior and expectations of individuals within a community. You want the child not to act as you please. Thus, one could argue that the child lacks freedom.

If the child accepts your dominion, he or she will also lose his sense of free will. To possess boundless freedom, an individual would need to have a keen sense of free will. If an individual were to possess a sense of free will, then he or she would not require freedom.

This proposition may appear paradoxical, if not nonsensical, but underscores the crux of a legal obligation. People believe that they have an obligation to the law because they can reason. That is, they understand their obligation to the law through their ability to reason. However, this is illogical.

The capacity to reason would produce the opposite effect, as obedience demands the individual to defer their intrinsic self to that of an external entity, who has dominion, not only on their way of life but also on their right to exist altogether. No reasonable entity would surrender to such an unreasonable demand or expectation. Hence, laws must also be enforced and reinforced.

This argument counters the concept of obligation, at least when considering it through the lens of reason. Pure reason would invalidate any sense of obligation in a reasonable individual. Thus, pure reason does not generate a sense of obligation to the law. The ability to reason can pose an obstacle to obligation. Imposing a specific form of reasoning can instigate a sense of universality. This fosters the need for conformity.

An obligation might stem from this enforced conformity, reinforced by laws and social norms. As previously emphasized, the obligation to the law is fundamentally a political obligation. With that in mind, there is more to the concept of obligation. Let us dive deeper into this topic.

CHAPTER 11

Natural and Positive Laws

Obligation is an alien notion within the confines of the natural world. As a species, humans strive primarily to fulfill their innate desires. This suggests that any form of obligation is far from their natural inclinations. It is as if obligations are not inherently part of human nature. Therefore, the assertion that an obligation is inherently nonnatural becomes a valid argument.

When humans face the raw forces of nature, their inherent instinct is to resist the elements using their most basic survival strategies. It is in their nature to adapt, evolve, and face adversities, whether physical, mental, or psychological. However, many aspects of the natural world remain beyond the grasp and control of human capabilities.

In contrast, when it comes to interpersonal dynamics, the situation becomes much more convoluted. Humans have an innate understanding of their kind. They may find it challenging, if not impossible, to ward off the influence exerted by others.

Over time, humans have developed a propensity for self-subordination. Present-day humans display a level of pliability that leads some to believe that they can shape the species specifically. This belief is prevalent among the scientific community, with many scientists convinced of their ability to influence human development in multiple directions.[1]

Although it appears that humans are susceptible to manipulation, it is important to state that they are not innately submissive. The consciousness of a human being is as untamed as that of nature itself. This reality suggests that if humans stay in tune with their inherent nature, no one can tame them.[2] There are instances where humans are compelled to abandon their natural state. Typically, in such circumstances, coercion induces or enforces human subordination. Fear of physical harm or mental distress serves as the catalyst for such compelled submission.

It is inherent in humans to possess the potential for freedom within the natural environment. However, the freedom to which humans aspire within a social context is often contingent on the perspectives of other humans. The notion of freedom is a human invention. Of course, this fact does not negate the innate human desire for natural freedom, which persists despite the constraints of a social environment.

As a species, humans face a compelling conundrum. Although they are inherently unrestrained within the natural environment, they have also existed within social constructs for millennia. Humans remain subject to the social context in which they live.

---

[1] In this case, I am referring to the creation or the production of man at a molecular level (biological engineering or cloning), at an ontological level (psychological engineering), and at a social level (social engineering).

[2] See the text titled Cogito, Ergo Philosophus to learn more.

Society, by its nature, appears to be in contradiction with the natural world. Its primary aim is to inhibit natural instincts. Thus, society stands in stark opposition to nature. In such a setting, humans may struggle to realize fully their natural potential because of the constraints of this artificial environment, which is a product of human imagination and ingenuity. Yet, such confines force them to exist regardless of their proclivities to do so.

Deprive of Their Nature

In a social setting, society strips men of their intrinsic nature. They become subservient to the environment. This environment may dictate actions. It may influence a person's behaviors. However, this is not always the case. There was a time when men remained true to their essence. They did so before becoming objects of societal influence.

Society so deeply entrenches modern generations of men that conceiving their survival outside it seems inconceivable. This reality results in poignant irony. Society is antithetical to nature. People have replaced their fundamental need for freedom with a desire for perpetual coercion.

This transition stems from the presumption that humans, were they to attain absolute freedom, would be at a loss about their utilization. Is there any validity to this claim? It is plausible that this perception holds some truth.

Men perceive freedom as being conditioned by societal norms. What an individual perceives as freedom may not be under the understanding of another person. People often deem men as reclusive, either mentally or socially.

Chapter 11: Natural and Positive Laws

Society necessitates that men relinquish their natural proclivity of freedom in exchange for an artificial substitute. Until now, freedom, as understood in a natural context, has no resemblance to its societal counterpart. In fact, I would contend that the notion of social freedom is a fallacy. In the social context, freedom remains an elusive concept.

Freedom and society are fundamentally incompatible. The existence of society hinges on conformity, rigidity, and compliance, elements inherently antithetical to the concept of free will and choice. If society allowed individuals to exercise their natural inclinations, it would lose its identity.

The existence of society serves to suppress the natural tendencies of individuals. This reality gives rise to the concept of "social order." This term implies a departure from the chaotic state of nature. On the contrary, discussing freedom within the context of society can be intellectually confounding, if not blatantly misleading.

These two notions are mutually exclusive and perpetually at odds with each other. Even the controllers of the social system find themselves trapped within its confines. They may manipulate or circumvent aspects of the system, yet they remain subject to its overarching power. Although the concept of social freedom in the context of citizen obligation remains an enigma, certain facets warrant further exploration. To shed light on these nuances, let us explore the necessity of freedom within a societal framework.

The intention behind establishing the laws was to promote freedom within a societal context. However, the survival of this environment predicates on the curtailment of freedom, the bedrock of society being, in fact, restriction. Thus, the concept of social freedom is elusive. Its significance is intangible. The mere existence of a society inherently signifies a sacrifice of freedom.

We need to investigate the notion of freedom more deeply to understand this paradox.

Seeking Freedom

The notions of freedom and civilization are dichotomous. They cannot co-exist harmoniously. Freedom implies a lack of constraint. Meanwhile, civilization demands the adhesion to society's perception of freedom.

Civilization, by its inherent nature, does not pave the way for freedom. It is a transient construct, while human freedom, in its essence, is contingent on the social context. Freedom is a perception, an ideal, an intellectual illusion.

These concepts are incongruous, since civilization implies order and structure. People commonly assume that civilization inevitably fosters peace and harmony. They often associate nature with chaos and unpredictability. This belief posits that nature incites disorder, which breeds a growing state of anarchy. Such anarchy spurs a relentless struggle for survival among earthly species. This leads to oppression and suppression. Erosion affects freedom.

Freedom, in its essence, is ephemeral, a mental state, rather than a tangible condition. Some may argue that freedom transcends a simple state of existence in the physical world, thus rendering the concept of societal freedom an unattainable ideal. Only when there is a desire for freedom can freedom exist in its purest form. However, this state is purely psychological. Freedom, as perceived by humans, is futile for an entity that does not need it. Similarly, freedom becomes an evanescent concept for those who cannot perceive it beyond a mere state of mind.

Chapter 11: Natural and Positive Laws

Freedom is a complex conundrum in the natural world. Those who yearn for it seldom possess the means to attain it. Yet, those capable of manifesting it rarely find a compelling reason to do so. In the realm of nature, an entity can only sustain its freedom by depriving others of the same, often extending to distinct species.

Comprehending freedom outside the metaphysical domain requires an understanding of what mental seclusion entails. It is a level of conceptualization that only a handful of individuals can achieve. The majority struggle to envision freedom beyond the judgment of others. For most, freedom is synonymous with conforming to social norms. Thus, from their point of view, freedom outside the purview of others is nonexistent.

This understanding of freedom inherently has unmitigated flaws. It limits itself to a restricted understanding of the expansiveness of the world. It also cannot understand our own nature. Freedom, in its true essence, signifies an expansive state of existence.

The battle for freedom in the natural world is interspecific. For instance, a zebra enjoys freedom when no lions threaten its existence. In contrast, societal freedom depends on mutual agreement. Men grant each other freedom at the expense of their own or others. Therefore, only men have the power to rob other men of their freedom.

The pursuit of freedom in society often leads to conflict. Men strive to monopolize any entity that might compromise their freedom or their perception of it. This perpetual struggle paradoxically fuels the quest for peace.

For peace and harmony to prevail in a societal context, men must give up their innate drive for freedom. They must suppress their natural instincts to neutralize threats to their tranquility. Society promises that men will strive for their freedom, but does this make up the existence of freedom itself? I posit that this is not the case.

Implicit in this promise is the requirement for men to renounce their concept of freedom to experience a semblance of it. They must surrender to the sovereignty of society. This surrender leads to entering a social contract. That contract obliges obedience to social laws. Freedom within an artificial milieu requires men to give up willingly their natural freedom.

This conceptualization of freedom, as understood by men, is inherently paradoxical. How can freedom exist within restrictive confines? Is it possible to experience true freedom in a constrained environment? I would say that is not the case. However, this concept of freedom forms the bedrock of society. Is it not that idea inherently ILLOGICAL?

Origin of Legal Obedience

Misconceptions about social norms and values gave rise to the notion of a legal obligation. While morality dictates human behavior in a social environment, it is often the case that a political obligation supersedes a moral obligation.

Consider the obligation to pay church dues versus the duty to pay taxes. The distinction between obligation and restriction emerges clearly here. It is not necessarily the case that one must do what one is expected to do. It is not necessarily the case that one must avoid an act or a conduct, which is prohibited. However, there persists an underlying assumption of an inherent obligation to abide by the law.

Viewed from an epistemological perspective, natural law and positive law bear a certain resemblance, particularly through a doctrinal lens. The subtle differences that the advocates of each

Chapter 11: Natural and Positive Laws

doctrine strive to establish lack a substantial intellectual foundation. There is a symbiotic relationship between these two approaches. Each approach is vital to establishing meaning. They rely on each other to function.

When viewed practically or politically, nonetheless, a discernible disparity emerges between the two terminologies. The laws of nature and the laws of men do not mirror each other. Each possesses unique intellectual properties. These properties produce different analytical approaches.

The advocacy of both natural law and positive law in unison is untenable. Their simultaneous existence is impossible. The laws of nature are immutable. Their effects on fundamental rights, human or otherwise, are inalienable.

Unrestrictive and universal in application, the laws of nature make no exceptions. Human existence does not supersede nature; every human being possesses the right to live within the natural world. From birth until death and beyond, nature provides for the individual.

In stark contrast, the laws of men exert unique, alienable effects on fundamental human rights. Engaging in natural conduct considered immoral or illegal (that is, a crime[3]) may result in deprivation of essential rights. This person could face death, loss of freedom, or reduced living conditions in a subhuman condition. Undeniably, the laws of men are inherently destructive.

To emphasize the arguments echoed here thus far, let us say that the laws of nature are fundamentally constructive. They promote harmonious coexistence among natural entities.

---

[3] Bear in mind that a crime is an act, a conduct, or a comportment that is defined as such by members of society. The concept is capricious and arbitrary at its core.

Unbound and universal, they offer men an uninhibited existence within the natural world, although humans do not dominate it. The same is not true for positive laws.

The Capricious Nature of the Law

The laws of men, or positive laws, are selectively applicable. They have certain exceptions that depend on the specific social context in which they apply them. This means that every law created by human societies inherently has a coercive nature, even though the extent of this coercion may vary.

Positive law cannot stand alone as a legal doctrine; it needs the foundation of natural law. However, there are challenges to discerning these two types of law. First, interpretations of natural law often resemble concepts of positive law. Second, the fundamental principles of positive law do not align with the natural environment.

Laws created by human societies are not independent or unique; they originate from maxims of natural law. However, the existing literature often cannot represent the true meaning of "natural law."

This calls for a reevaluation of the concept known as natural law. If we use natural law as the basis for explaining legal obligations, we must clearly distinguish between natural law and positive law. In addition, it is important to recognize that nature does not require human beings to obey each other. From this perspective, there is no natural obligation to abide by manufactured laws.

People often misunderstand the terms "positive law" and "natural law." It is important to draw a clear distinction between the laws of nature and the laws of men. While the laws of nature are innately compulsory, compliance is part of our instinct. The laws of men, in contrast, induce an obligation. Coercion enforces this obligation because our instincts do not naturally embed it. The distinction draws attention to fundamental differences in how diverse types of law is enforced and their nature. It also prompts an exploration of how human-made laws attempt to govern behavior, sometimes in contradiction with natural inclinations, and the ethical considerations that arise from such efforts.

SECTION 4

THE NATURE OF OBLIGATION

CHAPTER 12

Inherency in Legal Obligation

There is a pervasive assumption that individuals inherently desire to be part of a societal construct; that humankind is innately virtuous and is inclined to adhere to societal regulations. Advocates of this perspective frequently argue that humankind possesses a rational nature. These proponents propose that men aim for a higher level of behavioral standards within the natural order and, by implication, within society.

My position diverges from this perspective. Still, I acknowledge the potential existence of an obligation to obey the laws. Yet, I must note that such an obligation does not naturally arise from the essence of a human being.

Inherence suggests a natural inclination or an uncontrollable action. However, the invocation of nature as a justification for obedience to manufactured laws is questionable. The compliance to societal laws by men is necessary because of their existence within society. Specific territories confine most artificial laws.

Natural laws encompass all aspects of nature. Yet, nature lacks boundaries. It is omnipresent. However, the laws that apply in one area apply universally. We emphasize that geographical demarcations and cultural limitations restrict the laws of man.

Take, for example, the laws of Canada, which do not extend to the United States. The understanding here is that citizens of Canada are exempt from laws effective on American soil, despite the presumption of their reasonable nature. Similarly, Canadian laws do not influence citizens of the United States. American laws have no impact on Canadian citizens, at least within the confines of their respective territories. Therefore, the notion of an inherent obligation in the laws of two different countries or territories is not applicable.

Even international laws have limitations concerning their applicability and the entities they affect. An international organization cannot compel a country that does not participate in an agreement to comply with its regulations. For example, the United States often refrains from international agreements that may supersede their domestic laws.

Fear of subjugation to international laws is a recurring concern among American leaders. When we discuss inherent legal obedience, we typically use the term in its broadest sense. However, legal obedience has a scant or even negligible correlation with obligation.

Reason and Legal Obligation

A central misconception in the ongoing discourse on legal obligations is the notion of reason attributed to humans. Over centuries, philosophers and other scholars have used the term "reason" as a synonym of consciousness in humans. The underlying assumption is that the capacity to reason endows humans with the ability to distinguish right from wrong. Thus, they are able to differentiate between good and evil. They claim that a man has autonomy over his actions.

The prevalent conviction suggests that virtuous individuals always obey the law, while those with malevolent intentions disregard the law and behave irrationally. The phrase "a law-abiding citizen" is of vital importance in social contexts. Every individual resists the label of an "outlaw,' a term that carries the connotations of crime and negative behavior. The consensus states that good people do not engage in criminal activities.

The prospect of social condemnation discourages anyone from assuming the label of an outlaw. Detrimental repercussions arise from such a perception. They might lead to the deprivation of a person's natural rights. Society typically enforces rigorous penalties on those perceived as outlaws. This practice creates a deterrent for potential lawbreakers. It provides powerful incentives to obey the law.

The law can strip an individual of her natural rights. That person can be labeled an outlaw. She might lose her freedom or any semblance of it. Her life could also be at risk. Society incarcerates and, sometimes, inflicts capital punishment on individuals deemed as outlaws.

A peculiar predicament arises when the law violator is also the law enforcer. How would the situation unfold if the entity responsible for the creation of the law sought to dismantle it under the pretext that the law threatened the existence of the entity? These are some of the queries that generate negligible objective responses.

Being Above the Law

Imagine John Smith driving on a highway. He is exceeding the posted speed limit. There is a sense of urgency in his driving. A state trooper flags him down. At this point, Smith lacks the

Chapter 12: Inherency in Legal Obligation

freedom to abandon the command of the trooper. His failure to comply could lead to his arrest or, in extreme cases, to his loss of life. Smith must adhere to police directives, or he risks facing dire consequences. In this situation, obedience is the product of the absolute authority of the trooper or the widespread presence of the law (that is, the state's power).

Obeying the law is always advisable. The incentives associated with adhering to the law often surpasses the reasons for disobedience. In addition, people desire identification as law-abiding citizens rather than possessing a criminal history. Perceiving someone as a virtuous individual brings advantages that outweigh the disadvantages associated with the reputation of an outlaw.

To recap the central argument of the literary discourse, which is presented in the present edition, obedience is not an innate characteristic of humans. And so, citizens have no choice but to comply. Is this argument persuasive enough to align you with this perspective? I hope so. If not, let us delve further into the debate.

The points of view expressed so far revolve around the premise that the necessity of coercion signifies the absence of an inherent legal obligation. Induced obedience is necessary because of the requirement to enforce laws. The fact that the law obliges citizens to comply shows that the legal obligation is fundamentally unnatural.

Let us alter the trajectory of our discussion. Delving deeper into the nature of laws, let us investigate further. Let us examine the term "natural law" from the perspectives of various legal theorists.

Keep in mind that the ensuing two chapters will continue to address the concept of obligation. But recall the diverse perspectives from which we can interpret the term, "obligation." Let us explore how much we can impose on the populace.

CHAPTER 13

Assessing Natural Law

The concept of natural law derives from nature itself. This is evident in the concept's name. The term implies the laws of nature. It forms the junction between law and morality. This type of law, frequently viewed as the embodiment of reason,[1] is fundamentally an offshoot of moral theory, whereby a person reasons because one has a moral sense, which symbolizes one's adhesion to what is good or what is right.

As the law of reason, obedience to the law epitomizes the point of intersection between law and morality.[2] Therefore, people often describe the natural law theory as a moral theory.[3] The basis for this interpretation arises from the notion that nature endows everyone with an inherent ability to reason.

---

[1] Budziszewski, *Written on the Heart*.

[2] Raymond Wacks, *The Philosophy of Law: A Very Short Introduction* (Oxford ; New York: Oxford University Press, 2006).

[3] Jacques Maritain, *Natural Law: Reflections On Theory & Practice*, ed. William Sweet, 1 edition (South Bend, Ind: St. Augustines Press, 2001).

The central assertion of natural law pertains to the understanding of what is natural, or what should be.[4] The underlying belief is that reason equips a person with the ability to distinguish right from wrong. Natural law is universal; it is unwritten.[5] Unwritten and universal, natural law signifies what "does and ought to serve as a standard for human behavior."[6]

The predominant interpretation of natural law is that it evolves from the idea that we infer specific behaviors from nature through a mental process known as "reason." Hans Kelsen observes that natural law is not created by the act of a human will; it is not the artificial, arbitrary product of man.[7] It is the result of a natural progression.

The key principle of natural law is the concept of reason. The hypothesis is that since all humans possess the ability to reason, they can comprehend the natural law. If all humans can reason, it is assumed that "all people should respect" or should comply with natural law.[8]

John Finnis further remarks that the theory of natural law aims to "identify conditions and principles of practical right-mindedness, of good and proper order among persons, and in individual conduct."[9] Given this interpretation, it is presumed that humans can comprehend their natural rights through reason.

---

[4] Wacks, *The Philosophy of Law*.

[5] Maritain, *Natural Law*.

[6] Wacks, *The Philosophy of Law*, 7.

[7] Hans Kelsen, *General Theory of Law And State*, 1 edition (Clark, N.J: The Lawbook Exchange, Ltd., 2007), 9.

[8] Maritain, *Natural Law*, 7.

[9] John Finnis, *Natural Law and Natural Rights*, 2 edition (Oxford ; New York: Oxford University Press, 2011), 18.

The "law" presented by nature comes from an external source, such as God. This source imposes moral duties. It stipulates the rights that all humans should have. However, men's laws or positive laws can communicate such a divine law.

Regardless of God's dictation, we consider a law that is not natural as positive. These laws, as interpreted from the scriptures, require enforcement. This enforcement duty falls to an endogenous entity within the species, in this case: humankind. Therefore, the enforcement of these laws is inherently arbitrary. Let us further delve into the concept of positive law.

Assessing Positive Law

The term "positive law" commonly denotes the human influence on lawmaking. Derived from the verb "posit," the concept implies an imposition or setting. This term denotes that human minds create laws. This approach deals with synthetic laws. It refers to laws that humans introduce or impose onto their society.[10]

Advocates of positive law typically strive to delineate what is right and what is wrong. They propose, through the lens of justice, that humans have the capability to establish a positive legal order.[11] However, it is essential to highlight that positive law is different from positivism.[12]

Positive law refers to codifying legal rules and regulations that govern behavior within a specific jurisdiction. Positivism, by

---

[10] Wacks, *The Philosophy of Law*.

[11] Kelsen, *General Theory of Law And State*.

[12] Heinrich A. Rommen, *The Natural Law*, First edition (Indianapolis: Liberty Fund Inc., 1998).

contrast, is a philosophical approach that emphasizes empirical observation and scientific methodology, particularly within the realm of legal studies. The distinction between these two concepts underscores the complexity of legal terminology and the importance of precise language in the analysis and discussion of legal principles.

Positive law does not engender obligation from a void; at least, it does not create obligation from scratch.[13] This statement emphasizes that we do not construct legal obligations arbitrarily. They often emerge from preexisting social norms, ethical principles, or shared community values. The formation of legal obligations therefore involves a complex interplay between law, society, and human psychology. It suggests that the success and legitimacy of legal rules depend, in part, on their alignment with broader cultural understandings and expectations.

Positive law is based on natural law. For numerous legal positivists, such as Jeremy Bentham, there is no connection between positive and natural law. Bentham contends that the unwritten conventional law (that is, natural law) is too ambiguous to impose any standards for human behavior. Thus, the natural law, according to Bentham, cannot dictate any obligation. It is also important to note that other legal positivists perceive law as a series of commands, norms, rules, and institutional practices.[14]

---

[13] Ibid.

[14] Wacks, *The Philosophy of Law*.

Natural Law Versus Positive Law

Many academicians postulate that positive legal doctrines and conceptions of natural law should exist separately.[15] However, the exact nature of this "separation of positive laws and their merit or demerit leaves much to be desired."[16] Positive law focuses on notions of will and authority, while natural law lays emphasis on moral principles. The question arises whether there is a distinction between the two. From my perspective, there is no difference at all.

In affirming this understanding, I acknowledge that my viewpoint may not resonate universally. Observers typically engage in heated debates concerning the origins of manufactured laws rather than those around natural laws. However, the legitimacy of positive law theories is often subject to rigorous scrutiny.

Positive Law and Legal Obligation

As previously highlighted, in the context of obligation, the divide between natural and positive law is not clear, which some observers might consider blurred. We can examine both legal perspectives through the same analytical lens. Austin indicates a

---

[15] John Austin, *Austin: The Province of Jurisprudence Determined*, ed. Wilfrid E. Rumble, 1st edition (Cambridge ; New York, NY: Cambridge University Press, 1995); John Austin, *The Province of Jurisprudence Determined and The Uses of the Study of Jurisprudence* (Indianapolis, IN: Hackett Publishing Company, Inc., 1998); H. L. A. Hart et al., *The Concept of Law*, 3 edition (Oxford, United Kingdom: Oxford University Press, 2012).

[16] Hutchinson, *The Province of Jurisprudence Democratized*, 66.

"senseless differentiation between laws that are natural and positive."[17]

Such a viewpoint implies that a law can either be positive or natural. However, even if this were to be the case, I vehemently reject the assertion that all laws are natural. The natural law, as currently understood, extends beyond the positive law. All forms of law that humans create or enforce inherently bear human influence. I would make the argument that humans create all laws as positive rules. That way, I would also content, divine guidance may or may not influence them.

John Austin argues that we can categorize positive human laws into two types. The first type includes rules derived from morality. These apply to all humanity, and compliance is based on divine commandments. This categorization by Austin highlights the connection between legal principles and moral or religious beliefs. It reflects the ongoing debate within legal philosophy about the sources of law and the relationship between legal authority and moral or divine imperatives. The interpretation and application of such laws can lead to complex discussions about ethics, human rights, and the role of religious beliefs in secular legal systems.

The second type of positive human laws, as described by John Austin, includes rules that lack universality. An infallible authority does not guide compliance with these rules, such as a divinity.[18] Human institutions create laws that this category recognizes, and they are specific to societies or cultures. Unlike universal moral laws, these rules can vary widely between

---

[17] Austin, *The Province of Jurisprudence Determined and The Uses of the Study of Jurisprudence*, 102.

[18] Ibid.

different jurisdictions and reflect the unique values, traditions, and needs of a community.

The distinction between these two types of law illustrates the complex nature of legal systems and raises significant questions about the sources of legal authority, the role of cultural diversity in law, and the challenges of reconciling different legal traditions in a globalized world. Hans Kelsen further highlights a duality between positive and natural law.[19] He argues that natural law theory is incomplete as it cannot delineate right from wrong.

As it stands, natural law cannot clarify the overarching principle of justice. It does not delineate the conceptualization, which requires all humans to uphold a higher behavioral standard. The laws of nature are neither just nor legal; they are simply natural.

Positive law only exists where it aligns with natural law, but it resides outside the natural environment.[20] Such laws inherently contradict nature. Therefore, they are fundamentally inhumane.

Rommen emphasizes a mutual relationship between natural law and positive law.[21] From this perspective, the interpretation involves several dimensions. Foremost, 'natural law reappears whenever the positive law is transformed into objective injustice.[22] This transformation can occur "through the evolution and play"[23] of "vital forces" within society. That is, "the functional changes of communities"[24] can lead to this

---

[19] Kelsen, *General Theory of Law And State*.

[20] Ibid.

[21] Rommen, *The Natural Law*.

[22] Ibid., 230–31.

[23] Ibid.

[24] Ibid.

Chapter 13: Assessing Natural Law

reappearance of natural law. Put differently, "Natural law reappears whenever the positive law is transformed into objective injustice through the evolution and play and vital forces and the functional changes of communities."[25] The statement provides a nuanced view of the relationship between natural and positive law. It suggests dynamic interaction. This interplay is an intricate and complex phenomenon.

The text highlights how changes in social structures and community functions can influence the perception and implementation of law. These changes can alter the view and enforcement of the law. They can cause changes between the principles of natural law and the codified rules of positive law. Despite the previous understanding, one could argue that a legal chasm separates the concept of fabricated laws from notions related to the laws of nature.

---

[25] Ibid.

CHAPTER 14

A Legal Fissure

Could there be a chasm or disparity between natural law and positive law? Would legal theorists benefit from making [or even establishing] a distinction between natural and positive law? The answer would lean towards the negative.

What distinguishes these two notions? One approach to understand this reality is to recognize that moral queries permeate our existence, thereby becoming significant elements in political discourse.[1] One might also posit that evaluating legal obligation within society requires both perspectives.

The concept of normative law, as opposed to descriptive law also deserves attention as we wind down this discussion. As the nomenclature suggests, a normative approach to law stems from the belief that norms or values guide the formulation of laws. The presupposition here is that every individual should strive towards ideal behavior.

In the realm of morality, a normative interpretation of law proposes that humans should aspire towards a standard or prototype of behavior, achievable through reason. The assertion

---

[1] Wacks, *The Philosophy of Law*.

states that all humans can choose virtuous conduct over wrongful actions. Each human being could or should always know what it is or should be.

Joseph Raz examines the notion of a "norm" within the framework of authority.[2] The author suggests that norms are significant when considering the influence one individual may hold over another.[3] The proposition starts with the idea that we can comprehend obligation through the existence of a particular relationship. Specifically, this relationship involves "some mutually recognized normative relationship giving the one the right to command or speak."[4]

Concurrently, it provides "the other the duty to obey."[5] This concept emphasizes the mutual recognition and understanding between parties, where one has the authority to direct, and the other has the responsibility to follow. This idea is fundamental in the exploration of legal and ethical relationships. It underscores the dynamics of power within social interactions. In addition, it highlights the elements of authority and responsibility within these interactions. Put differently, the proposition is that we can understand obligation in terms of the existence of "some mutually recognized normative relationship giving the one the right to command or speak and the other the duty to obey."[6]

A distinct boundary between natural law and a normative approach to law is scarcely discernible. What pertains to one

---

[2] Joseph Raz, ed., *Authority* (New York: NYU Press, 1990).

[3] Ibid.

[4] Ibid.

[5] Ibid.

[6] Ibid.

approach is not necessarily like the other. A normative lens best views the legitimacy of authority within the context of obligation.

What is the law, really?

There is no singular methodology capable of effectively articulating the law. The description of what law encompasses can vary, depending on specific legal domains. Brian Bix illustrates that Hart's approach to inquiries about law is framed by the question, "why do you ask?"[7] This question helps to set the context for understanding the nature of legal inquiry.

The implication that follows is that the meaning of law may be relegated to "the proper descriptions of our practices."[8] This suggests that law's meaning can be found in how it is applied and understood within a particular social context. Hart's perspective emphasizes the importance of the practical application of law, rather than abstract definitions or universal principles.

A comprehensive understanding of the nature of law or the foundational aspects of legal concepts cannot be obtained without considering the social, political, moral, and economic dimensions of various theoretical concepts.[9] Raymond Wacks suggests that grasping the improbable task of deciphering the concept of legal obligation necessitates an understanding of the rudiments of law or legal systems. If these understandings hold, we should not approach the concept from a superficial perspective.

---

[7] Bix, *Jurisprudence*, 6.

[8] Ibid.

[9] Raymond Wacks, *Law: A Very Short Introduction*, 1 edition (Oxford ; New York: Oxford University Press, 2008).

Chapter 14: A Legal Fissure

What defines law, at least in the simplest sense? The answer remains elusive. What makes up the law that confounds most laypeople?

Even legal experts, as I contend, struggle to explain the complexity of legal notions. In jurisprudence, or legal theory, there is no shortage of relevant work on the fundamentals of the law. However, what makes up law at a philosophical level remains unclear to most thinkers.

Legal anthologies often incite numerous disputes. The controversy typically revolves around natural legal doctrines as opposed to positive law. However, which approach best clarifies the sources of laws or explains the rationale for obligation? I concede that the answer remains indeterminate.

Different Attitudes About the Law

Opinions often deviate when it comes to defining the law. However, disagreements in jurisprudence bear a significant resemblance to fundamental moral or political disputes present in society.[10] Perspectives concerning authority often ignite heated debates, just as those surrounding the notion of obligation find themselves subjected to rigorous scrutiny. These viewpoints constantly undergo meticulous examination.

Some scholars claim a proprietary understanding of legal concepts. However, legal notions, such as citizen obedience, are often construed through a distorted lens. The crux of the issue lies in the fact that our knowledge of the law remains limited. This limitation results in a restricted understanding of authority. It also leads to a reduced grasp of obligation. Such a confined

---

[10] Bix, *Jurisprudence*.

comprehension of citizen obligation inadvertently fortifies misguided notions about the law itself.

In the field of law, there are varying perspectives. They bring to the forefront various interpretations. Each interpretation offers a unique view of what makes up law. These dissimilar viewpoints, interestingly, mirror the debates and disagreements that are commonly found in societal moral or political discourse. Opinions surrounding the concept of authority tend to trigger intense discussions. Similarly, perspectives related to the notion of obligation are often contentious and constantly subject to meticulous critique and examination.

A group of scholars, as we see, claims a proprietary understanding of certain legal concepts. One such notion that often falls into this domain is citizen obedience. However, it is important to emphasize that these interpretations are frequently framed through a distorted or limited perspective. The issue here arises from the broader problem of our collective understanding of the law being inherently limited. This constrained comprehension, in turn, results in a narrow view of topics such as authority and obligation.

This restricted understanding of the citizen's obligation has downstream effects, inadvertently bolstering flawed assumptions about the law itself. It often fosters and reinforces misconceptions while inhibiting a broader, more comprehensive understanding of the legal system. This reality can perpetuate biases, misjudgments, and an often-oversimplified view of complex legal dynamics. Therefore, it is essential to strive for a deeper, more holistic understanding of these concepts, both within legal academia and in societal discourse at large.

Chapter 14: A Legal Fissure

Wrapping Up This Treatise

The intent of this discourse was to investigate the elusive remnants of the inherent obligation in the duty to obey the law. After extensive research in the literature, I find myself still at odds with the concept of legal obedience. In other words, I remain unconvinced of the existence of any innate obligation within the law or related to the law.

It strikes me as improbable that humans are inherently predisposed to exist according to the decrees of others. A law [in itself] does not instill obedience in individuals; rather, it requires compulsion for its enforcement. The law serves as a legitimizing tool for such coercion. Although the necessity of laws in societal contexts might be difficult to dispute, we must grapple with the underlying premise of legal obedience.

Without a doubt, humans are prone to the power of suggestion. Whether this is an admirable or undesirable trait was not the focal point of this examination. I contend that humans naturally do not have a proclivity for goodness or evil.

We do not inherently judge what we classify as good or evil. We must instill the concepts of righteousness. During this analysis, my endeavor has been to illuminate that the legal obligation does not arise from nature. I proposed applying two distinct perspectives to this concept.

The first perspective attributes the motivation for behavior to nature itself. Humans can reason. Individuals can manifest this ability by embracing norms and values over time.

The second perspective emphasizes the idea of positive law: Human beings formulate and enforce these laws. Following this logic, we can discern the inherent nature of individuals based on their adherence to established behavioral standards. However, the issue is more complex than that.

Modern perceptions of nature tend to be far from accurate. The divide between these two perspectives is non-existent. Humankind imprints its hand indelibly on both natural law and positive law. As a result, humans play an identical role in both perspectives. Humans significantly influence their environment and social structures, and this testament proves this.

Who decides which values society should uphold? Who establishes the institutions that enforce these values and appoint those who will do the enforcement? The authority to legislate and the power to demand absolute obedience from citizens may not have a natural origin.

Obligation is always affirmative, always articulated. As a separate thought rather than a conclusion, I argue that society posits every law. However, certain moral perspectives also root for such a stance. Contextual understandings of what justice is or should be, in turn, shape these perspectives.

Theologically, social groups decide the nature of morality, its perception, and the individuals responsible for it. We cannot refer to the natural tendency of human beings to adhere to unnatural laws or synthetic rules. The only reasonable conclusion is that social laws are obligatory, either politically or morally.

That obligation is induced through coercion, which can be by using power (the threat thereof) or through sheer brute force (or the threat thereof). The notion that peoples obey the law because of their inherent predisposition to do the same is absurd, to say the least. This reality is the foundation of citizen obedience.

Chapter 14: A Legal Fissure

FINAL WORDS

CONCLUDING THOUGHTS

Conclusions

I thank you for accompanying me throughout this fascinating intellectual tête-à-tête. Throughout this thought-provoking exploration of an important reality in modern societies, we have delved deeply into the realms of natural law. We have also explored positive laws. In both areas, we have attempted to discern the inherent obligations within these fields. The aim was to disentangle, as much as possible, the subtle complexities involved in our understanding of law, the different facets of which illuminate both its natural and manufactured components.

Our journey started with the concepts of positive law and natural law. Initial contentions on the subject sparked a much discussion about the inherent relationship and distinction between the two philosophies. The challenge was to understand if there was a palpable distance or a fissure between these two elements of jurisprudence.

We explore the following questions: Does there exist a clear delimitation exist between moral imperatives and legally enforced rules? Otherwise, are these principles two sides of the same coin? To this end, we analyzed these doctrinal understandings, which such inquiries should not be examined in isolation. Rather, we must consider their sociopolitical, economic, and moral dimensions.

The role of norms and values, intrinsic to human beings, in shaping laws was another compelling facet we examined. With the ability to reason, human beings can choose between good and bad behaviors, thus enforcing an ideal conduct through the law.

Conclusions

Our exploration included the critical work of various scholars, including Joseph Raz and John Austin.

Joseph Raz provided insight into norms and authority. He emphasized the relationship between legal systems and moral values. His work provided a deep understanding of how these two aspects are interrelated. John Austin's contributions focused on the differentiation and interplay between natural and positive law. He provided an analytical framework for understanding the nature of legal rules. This involved distinguishing between universal laws and laws guided by morality.

Correspondingly, there was a focus on those laws that are specific to jurisdictions. Together, the work of these scholars illuminates various aspects of legal theory. They shed light on the complexities of norms. They also explore the intricacies of authority and examine the relationship between distinct types of law. Their viewpoints contribute to a richer understanding of legal principles. This reflects the multifaceted nature of legal inquiry. Different perspectives bring depth and variety to the understanding of these principles.

As we move forward, discussions about the nature and meaning of law and the challenges faced by lay people and experts in comprehending its nuances came to the fore. There is broad agreement that our understanding of law is neither static nor straightforward. Interpretations often diverge because of context and perspective.

In our quest to understand the inherent obligation to obey the law, we question the premise of legal obedience. We posited that laws do not induce obedience, but rather legitimize coercion. We dissected the notion that there is no inherent good or bad. Thus, we must teach righteousness, and a legal obligation does not naturally occur.

Finally, we conclude that we posit all social laws. We base their foundations on certain moral views. Yet, we derive these views from contextual understandings of justice. The decisive role of social groups in deciding the nature of morality, its perception, and the individuals responsible for it became evident. The dismissal was because of the idea that humans naturally adhere to unnatural or artificial laws. Instead, we showed how social laws were perceived as politically or morally obligatory through a compelling analysis.

This book serves not as a final statement on the matter, but rather as a starting point for further inquiry into the nuanced world of jurisprudence. The demarcation between natural law and positive law is not as stark as some may believe. In the same way, obligation is not simply a matter of inherent compliance but a more complex interplay of societal norms, individual reasoning, and the inherent need for order. As we move forward in our collective understanding of these concepts, we must remember that law, in any form, serves as a reflection of our societal values and aspirations. The pursuit of justice and understanding of our obligations continues.

To build upon the previous reflections, we can further scrutinize the multifaceted discourse around the relationship between natural and positive law. Our journey has explained that these doctrines, while theoretically distinct, converge and diverge in myriad ways. The dynamic nature of their interplay lends itself to the ongoing evolution of our understanding of legal systems and their role in society.

The foundational analysis suggested that the positive law is more explicit. It focuses on legislation created and enforced by men. Natural law introduces a moral dimension to our understanding of law. It emphasizes the inherent values and behaviors of humans. However, our discussions showed that the

Conclusions

line between these two doctrines is not clear. The imprints of men on both natural and positive law, their role in determining social values, and the institutions established for law enforcement blur this line further.

This understanding leads us to an intriguing facet of the law, the notion of obligation and obedience. Conversations in this book have argued against the inherent obligation to obey the law. The presentation of the argument stated that law does not inherently inspire obedience. Instead, it legitimates a form of coercion. Whether humans naturally comply with existing laws or whether enforcement drives such compliance is an important question.

This does not undermine the importance of law. Through this social construct, we mediate disputes, manage public affairs, protect individuals, and foster social order. Laws, whether grounded in natural law or positive law, reflect our collective moral compass and societal aspirations.

The discourse also challenges our preconceived notions about the inherent "goodness" or "badness" in humans, which proposes that righteousness is taught and learned, not innate. We intrinsically link this perspective to how we understand and engage with the law. This applies both in terms of our personal adherence and the societal norms we collectively agree to uphold.

Drawing these threads together, we understand that social laws are not inherently obedient. Thus, they always induce obedience, which must be to the detriment of the person faced with that choice or that decision. Instead, they are politically or morally obligatory. This realization emphasizes the critical role of social norms, moral values, and collective understandings in shaping our interaction with the law.

Several key aspects enrich our understanding of jurisprudence. The relationship between natural law and positive law reveals the intricacies of how universal principles and specific social rules ground legal concepts. Social norms shape our understanding of obligations, demonstrating the intertwining of legal obligations with cultural values and social expectations.

In the end, the ongoing debate on the inherent nature of obedience highlights the complexities of human behavior in relation to the law. This reality also reveals how obedience is not merely a mechanical response, but involves a nuanced interplay of beliefs, attitudes, and social context. These considerations offer a multifaceted view of the law. They reflect its complexity. They also highlight its deep connections with various aspects of human life and thought.

This book is a testament to the complexity of law. It urges us towards a more nuanced and critical understanding of its role and function in society. However, the dialogue around these themes does not end here.

This book serves as an invitation to engage, question, and explore these complex concepts. Encourage further reflection, debate, and understanding. In the ceaseless pursuit of justice and clarity in the realm of law, may we continue to engage critically and constructively with these enduring questions?

Conclusions

Bibliography

Augustyn, Megan Bears. "Updating Perceptions of (in) Justice." *Journal of Research in Crime and Delinquency* 53, no. 2 (2016): 255–86.

Austin, John. *Austin: The Province of Jurisprudence Determined*. Edited by Wilfrid E. Rumble. 1st edition. Cambridge ; New York, NY: Cambridge University Press, 1995.

———. *The Province of Jurisprudence Determined and The Uses of the Study of Jurisprudence*. Indianapolis, IN: Hackett Publishing Company, Inc., 1998.

Bix, Brian H. *Jurisprudence: Theory and Context*. Fifth edition. Durham, N.C: Carolina Academic Press, 2009.

Budziszewski, J. *Written on the Heart: The Case for Natural Law*. Downers Grove, Ill: IVP Academic, 1997.

Comins, Neil F. *Heavenly Errors: Misconceptions about the Real Nature of the Universe*. Columbia University Press, 2001.

Djatmiko, WP, Suteki Suteki, and Nyoman Putra Jaya. "Reconstruction Legal Culture of Madurese Based on Pancasila Values as Criminal Policy in Tackling Carol," 2019.

Dougherty, Daniel J, Kathi Fisler, and Shriram Krishnamurthi. "Obligations and Their Interaction with Programs," 375–89. Springer, 2007.

Estlund, David. "Political Authority and the Tyranny of Non-Consent." *Philosophical Issues* 15 (2005): 351–67.

Finnis, John. *Natural Law and Natural Rights*. 2 edition. Oxford ; New York: Oxford University Press, 2011.

Forman, Lisa, Gorik Ooms, Audrey Chapman, Eric Friedman, Attiya Waris, Everaldo Lamprea, and Moses Mulumba. "What Could a Strengthened Right to Health Bring to the Post-2015 Health Development Agenda?: Interrogating the Role of the Minimum Core Concept in Advancing Essential Global Health Needs." *BMC International Health and Human Rights* 13 (2013): 1–11.

Green, Leslie. "Legal Obligation and Authority." In *The Stanford Encyclopedia of Philosophy*, edited by Edward N. Zalta, Winter 2012. Metaphysics Research Lab, Stanford University, 2012. https://plato.stanford.edu/archives/win2012/entries/legal-obligation/.

Guryanov, Alexei Sergeyevich, Elina Borisovna Minnullina, and Alfred Ildarovich Shakirov. "Kantian Ethics: The Phenomena Of Respect And Worth (Worthiness)," 675–82, 2021. https://doi.org/10.15405/epsbs.2021.11.89.

Hart, H. L. A., Leslie Green, Joseph Raz, and Penelope A. Bulloch. *The Concept of Law*. 3 edition. Oxford, United Kingdom: Oxford University Press, 2012.

Hasnas, John. "Is There a Moral Duty to Obey the Law?" *Social Philosophy and Policy* 30, no. 1–2 (January 2013): 450–79. https://doi.org/10.1017/S0265052513000216.

Hilty, Manuel, David Basin, and Alexander Pretschner. "On Obligations," 98–117. Springer, 2005.

Hittinger, Russell. "Liberalism and the American Natural Law Tradition." *Wake Forest L. Rev.* 25 (1990): 429.

Hutchinson, Allan C. *The Province of Jurisprudence Democratized*. 1 edition. Oxford ; New York: Oxford University Press, 2008.

Hyams, Keith. "When Consent Doesn't Work: A Rights-Based Case for Limits to Consent's Capacity to Legitimise." *Journal of Moral Philosophy* 8, no. 1 (2011): 110–38.

Johnson, Ben Wood. *Cogito, Ergo Philosophus: I Think, Therefore I Philosophize*. Tesko Publishing, 2019.

———. *Natural Law: Morality and Obedience*. Eduka Solutions, 2017.

Kelsen, Hans. *General Theory of Law And State*. 1 edition. Clark, N.J: The Lawbook Exchange, Ltd., 2007.

Kotlán, Pavel, Alena Kozlová, and Zuzana Machová. "Opening a Path towards Sustainable Corporate Behaviour: Public

Participation in Criminal Environmental Proceedings." *Sustainability* 13, no. 14 (2021): 7886.

Krupka, Erin L., Stephen Leider, and Ming Jiang. "A Meeting of the Minds: Informal Agreements and Social Norms." *Management Science*, May 31, 2016. https://doi.org/10.1287/mnsc.2016.2429.

Latapí Agudelo, Mauricio Andrés, Lára Jóhannsdóttir, and Brynhildur Davídsdóttir. "A Literature Review of the History and Evolution of Corporate Social Responsibility." *International Journal of Corporate Social Responsibility* 4, no. 1 (2019): 1–23.

Lee, Constance Youngwon. "Calvinist Natural Law and the Ultimate Good,"." *The Western Australian Jurist* 5 (2014): 153–75.

Lischka, Mario. "Dynamic Obligation Specification and Negotiation," 155–62. IEEE, 2010.

Manson, Neil C. "Normative Consent Is Not Consent." *Cambridge Quarterly of Healthcare Ethics* 22, no. 1 (2013): 33–44.

Maritain, Jacques. *Natural Law: Reflections On Theory & Practice*. Edited by William Sweet. 1 edition. South Bend, Ind: St. Augustines Press, 2001.

McAdams, Richard H., and Janice Nadler. "Coordinating in the Shadow of the Law: Two Contextualized Tests of the Focal Point Theory of Legal Compliance." *Law & Society Review* 42, no. 4 (December 2008): 865–98. https://doi.org/10.1111/j.1540-5893.2008.00361.x.

Meirovitch, Yaron, Hila Harris, Eran Dayan, Amos Arieli, and Tamar Flash. "Alpha and Beta Band Event-Related Desynchronization Reflects Kinematic Regularities." *Journal of Neuroscience* 35, no. 4 (2015): 1627–37.

Michel, Jeremy J, Eileen Erinoff, and Amy Y Tsou. "More Guidelines than States: Variations in US Lead Screening and Management Guidance and Impacts on Shareable CDS Development." *BMC Public Health* 20 (2020): 1–10.

Milgram, Stanley, and Christian Gudehus. "Obedience to Authority," 1978.

Morrison, Elizabeth Wolfe, and Sandra L Robinson. "When Employees Feel Betrayed: A Model of How Psychological Contract Violation Develops." *Academy of Management Review* 22, no. 1 (1997): 226–56.

Murphy, Mark C. "Philosophical Anarchisms, Moral and Epistemological." *Canadian Journal of Law & Jurisprudence* 20, no. 1 (2007): 95–111.

Oosterhoff, Benjamin, Natalie J. Shook, Russ Clay, and Aaron Metzger. "Differential and Domain-Specific Associations Among Right-Wing Authoritarianism, Social Dominance Orientation, and Adolescent Delinquency." *Personality and Social Psychology Bulletin*, June 22, 2017. https://doi.org/10.1177/0146167217711937.

Papachritos, Adrew V, Tracey L Meares, and Jeffrey Fagan. "Why Do Criminals Obey the Law-the Influence of Legitimacy and Social Networks on Active Gun Offenders." *J. Crim. L. & Criminology* 102 (2012): 397.

Raz, Joseph, ed. *Authority*. New York: NYU Press, 1990.

Rommen, Heinrich A. *The Natural Law*. First edition. Indianapolis: Liberty Fund Inc., 1998.

Royakkers, Lambèr, and Jesse Hughes. "Blame It on Me." *Journal of Philosophical Logic* 49, no. 2 (2020): 315–49.

Saunders, Ben. "Normative Consent and Opt-out Organ Donation." *Journal of Medical Ethics* 36, no. 2 (2010): 84–87.

Sensoy, Murat, Timothy J Norman, Wamberto W Vasconcelos, and Katia Sycara. "OWL-POLAR: A Framework for Semantic Policy Representation and Reasoning." *Journal of Web Semantics* 12 (2012): 148–60.

Shelley, Catherine, and Catherine Shelley. "Natural Law, Reason and Religion." *Ethical Exploration in a Multifaith Society*, 2017, 59–91.

Todd, Emma G. *Discoveries of Misconceptions Regarding the Properties of Matter Within the Science of Chemistry*. Whitaker & Ray Company, 1898.

Wacks, Raymond. *Law: A Very Short Introduction*. 1 edition. Oxford ; New York: Oxford University Press, 2008.

———. *The Philosophy of Law: A Very Short Introduction*. Oxford ; New York: Oxford University Press, 2006.

Walton, Kevin. "The Particularities of Legitimacy: John Simmons on Political Obligation." *Ratio Juris* 26, no. 1 (2013): 1–15.

Wei, Lijun. "Construction of the Interactive Relationship between Law Enforcement and Legislation Based on the Background of Big Data." *Mathematical Problems in Engineering* 2022 (May 17, 2022): e6888268. https://doi.org/10.1155/2022/6888268.

Wu, Shuai, Tiansu Ren, Huan Xia, and Xiuzhang Yang. "Research on Sentiment Analysis of Public Opinion Events Based on Human Behavior Dynamics," 12260:541–49. SPIE, 2022.

Young, Kathryne M. "Everyone Knows the Game: Legal Consciousness in the Hawaiian Cockfight." *Law & Society Review* 48, no. 3 (2014): 499–530.

Zhu, Jiangnan, Huang Huang, and Dong Zhang. "'Big Tigers, Big Data': Learning Social Reactions to China's Anticorruption Campaign through Online Feedback." *Public Administration Review* 79, no. 4 (2019): 500–513.

Further Reading

Bastiat, F. (2007). *The law*. Auburn, Alabama: Ludwig von Mises Institute.

Denning, L. (1979). *The discipline of law*. Woburn, Massachusetts: terworth (Publishers) Inc.

Hill, N. G., Hill, T. K. (2009). *Nolo's plain-English law dictionary*. Berkeley, California: Delta Printing Solutions, Inc.

Patterson, D. (2003). *Philosophy of law and legal theory: an anthology*. Malden, MA: Blackwell Publishing Ltd.

Schmitt, C. (2005). Foreword by (Strong, B. T.). *Political theology: Four chapters on the concept of sovereignty.* (Schwab, G., Trans.). Chicago and London: The University of Chicago Press.

Simmons, A. J. (1979). *Moral principles and political obligations.* Princeton, New Jersey: Princeton University Press.

Simon, R. Y., (1993). *Philosophy of democratic government.* United States: First University of Notre Dame Press.

Spooner, L. (1882). Natural law; or the science of justice: A treatise on natural law, natural justice, natural rights, natural liberty, and natural society, showing that all legislation whatsoever is an absurdity, a usurpation, and a crime (Part First). Boston: A Williams & Co.

Tobin, P. C. (2007). *Twenty-five doctrines of law you should know.* New York, NY: Algora Publishing.

Wacks, R. (2009). *Understanding jurisprudence: An introduction to legal theory.* New York, New York: Oxford University Press Inc.

Index

Absolute, Absolute, 4, 23, 41, 43, 95, 108, 123, 139
   Absolute authority, 108, 139
Absoluteness, 29, 139
Abuse, 73–4, 81, 139
   Abuse of Authority, 81, 139
Acceptance, 29–30, 75, 139
Accountability, 31, 64–5, 71, 81, 139
   Accountability in Law Enforcement, 71, 139
Alien, 38, 93, 139
   Alienable, 100, 139
Antagonistic Scheme, 1, 139
Anthropomorphize, 54, 139
Appropriateness, 85, 139
Artificial, 3, 22–3, 32, 95, 99, 105, 110, 129, 139
   Artificial Environment, 95, 139
   Artificial Laws, 3, 22–3, 105, 129, 139
Attitude, 18, 120, 131, 139
Augustines, 109, 135
Authoritarianism, 14, 136
Authoritative, 13, 62
Authority, 3–4, 10–1, 14, 20, 27–8, 31, 38–9, 46, 51, 53–67, 69–72, 80–1, 91, 108, 113–5, 118–21, 123, 128, 133–6, 139, 142, 144
   Authority and Obedience, 91, 139
   Authority of Law Enforcement Officers, 69
Autocratic Rulers, 48, 139
Autonomous entity, 37, 139
Autonomy, 15, 20, 40, 106, 139, 144
Bad, 10, 127–8, 139
   Bad Behaviors, 127, 139
Bedrock, 28, 75, 96, 99, 139
   Bedrock of Society, 96, 99, 139
Behavior, 4, 11–2, 14, 38–9, 41, 57, 59, 62, 64, 66, 72–3, 75, 79–80, 86–7, 90–1, 95, 99, 102, 107, 110–2, 117, 122, 127, 129, 131, 137, 139, 141, 145
   Behavioral, 21, 105, 115, 122, 139
   Behavioral regulation, 21, 139
   Behavioral standards, 105, 122, 139
   Behavior norms, 57, 139
Belief, 4, 12, 15, 19, 22, 25–6, 28, 30, 38, 40–2, 46, 48, 73, 80, 86, 93, 97, 110, 114, 117, 131, 139, 145
   Believers, 45, 139
Bentham, Jeremy, 112, 142
Bias, 31, 73, 78, 121, 139, 141
   Biased, 139
Brute, 23, 50, 54, 57–9, 62, 123, 139
   Brute force, 23, 50, 54, 57–9, 123, 139
Budziszewski, 88, 109, 133, 139
Canada, 106, 139
   Canadian, 11, 106, 136, 139
Capital punishment, 50, 107, 139
Certainty, 21, 64, 139
Choice, 40, 43, 46, 50, 61, 75, 80, 82, 88, 96, 108, 130, 139
Church Dues, 99, 139
Citizen, 1–4, 9–11, 24–7, 33, 37–8, 41, 47–8, 50–1, 53, 59–60, 64–7, 69–75, 77–8, 80, 96, 106–8, 120–1, 123, 139, 142
   Citizen Obedience, 1–2, 24, 26, 37, 41, 78, 120–1, 123, 139
   Citizen rights, 3, 71, 139
   Citizenry, 3, 37, 67, 139
   Citizenship, 74, 139
Civil, 69–71, 74, 139
   Civil Rights, 69–71, 74, 139
Civilization, 38, 42, 97, 139
Codified norms, 62, 139
Coerced, 23, 139
Coercion, 46, 50, 58–60, 67, 77, 88–9, 94–5, 101, 108, 122–3, 128, 130, 139

Index

Coercive, 4, 54, 80, 90, 101, 139
   Coercive Force, 54, 139
   Coercive Nature, 101, 139
Collaboration, 62, 65, 139
Collective, 37, 54, 56–7, 63–4, 75, 87–9, 121, 129–30, 139–40
   Collective Conformity, 89, 139
   Collective entity, 37, 140
Command, 49, 59, 62, 65, 108, 112, 118, 140
   Commanding, 61–2, 140
   Commandments, 45, 114, 140
Community, 11, 14, 66, 69–70, 75, 91, 94, 112, 115–6, 140–1
   Community Involvement, 69, 140
Complex, 1, 13, 15, 24, 42, 51, 56–7, 61, 66–7, 70, 81–2, 86, 97, 112, 114–6, 121–2, 127–9, 131, 140
   Complexity, 9, 20–1, 55, 66, 77–8, 112, 120, 131, 140
   Complexity of Law, 77, 131, 140
Compliance, 2–4, 10–1, 13–5, 19, 23, 32, 51, 59–60, 65–7, 72, 74–5, 79–80, 89–90, 96, 101, 105, 114, 129–30, 135, 140, 142, 145
   Compliance with Societal Regulations, 72
Compulsion, 9, 38, 47, 67, 122, 140
Compulsive, 1, 140
Compulsory, 101, 140
Concept, 1, 4, 8–9, 11–2, 14, 18, 25–8, 32–3, 37–42, 53–4, 56–7, 61, 63–4, 66–8, 80, 82, 85–9, 91–2, 96–101, 108–13, 116–22, 127, 129, 131, 133–4, 138, 140, 142
   Conception, 25, 47, 113, 140
   Concept of Reason, 85–9, 110, 140
   Conceptualization, 63, 87, 98–9, 115, 140
Conduct, 10, 43, 49, 57, 90, 99–100, 110, 118, 127, 140–1, 145–6
   Conduct code, 43, 140
Conflict, 3, 62, 98
Conform, 9, 41, 89, 140
   Conforming, 98, 140
      Conformism, 30, 140
      Conformity, 18, 29–30, 48, 89–90, 92, 96, 139–40, 144
Conscience, 86, 140–1
   Consciousness, 10, 37, 94, 106, 137, 140
Consensus, 25, 27, 45–6, 87, 107, 140
Consent, 25–9, 134–6, 140, 144

Constraint, 9, 20, 40, 58, 80, 94–5, 97, 140–1
Contingent Truths, 88, 140
Contract, 7, 28, 47, 75, 99, 136, 140, 145
   Contract Law, 28, 140
   Contractual, 28, 140
Contradict, 32, 39, 80, 115, 140
   Contradiction, 32, 40, 42, 94, 102, 140, 143
   Contradictory, 79, 140
Cosmos, 21, 140
Crime, 11, 100, 107, 133, 138, 140
   Criminal, 8, 10, 26, 72, 107–8, 133, 135–6, 140
   Criminal activities, 107, 140
Critical Understanding, 131, 140
Culture, 10, 75, 114, 133, 140
   Cultural, 45, 64, 105, 112, 115, 131, 140
   Cultural Diversity, 115, 140
   Cultural Norms, 45, 64, 140
   Cultural Values, 131, 140
Deliberation, 88, 140
Democratic, 64, 67, 81, 138, 140
   Democratic society, 64, 140
Descriptive Law, 117, 140
Desire to Transcend, 29, 140
Deterrence, 59, 140
Deterrent, 79, 107, 140
Dialogue, 2, 63, 65, 70, 74, 131, 140
Dichotomous, 97
Discretion, 31, 50, 53, 57, 79, 82, 140
Discrimination, 49, 74, 140
Discriminatory Practices, 31, 69, 71–2, 140
Distinction between Natural and Positive Law, 117
Divine, 4, 23, 25, 41–2, 45–6, 111, 114, 140–1
   Divine Commandments, 45, 114, 140
   Divine Creator, 45–6, 140–1
   Divine inspiration, 42, 140
   Divine Law, 4, 111, 140
   Divine Origins, 25, 140
Divinity, 15, 18, 41, 57, 114, 140
Doctrinal Understandings, 127, 140
Doctrine, 3, 9, 19, 99, 101, 113, 120, 129–30, 138, 140, 142–3
Dogmatic susceptibilities, 42, 140
Dominion, 91, 140
Draconian Rules, 49, 140

Duty, 1–2, 4, 9, 13, 17–9, 29, 37–8, 40, 46–7, 66, 70, 73, 80, 82, 99, 111, 118, 122, 134, 140–1, 143, 145
Duty to Obey the Law, 13, 122, 134, 140
Dynamic, 9, 14, 20, 55–6, 61–2, 64–70, 72, 85, 91, 93, 116, 118, 121, 129, 135, 137, 140, 142, 144
Dynamics of power, 56, 61, 64, 70, 118, 140
Economic Dimensions, 119, 140
Education, 65, 75, 87, 140
Effectiveness, 3, 10, 12, 73, 140
Emancipation, 42, 47, 140–1
Emotional arguments, 43, 140
Emotional Reactions, 1, 140
Empirical Validation, 27, 140
Enduring Questions, 131, 140
Enforcement, 3, 11–2, 22, 31, 47, 50–1, 53, 55, 64–7, 69–75, 77–9, 81–2, 111, 116, 122–3, 130, 137, 139, 141–2, 144
Enforcement Duty, 111, 141
Enforcement mechanism, 64, 141
Equity, 18, 68, 141
Equitable, 64, 66–7, 81, 141
Equitable Application of Laws, 81, 141
Equitable enforcement, 64, 141
Ethics, 14, 28, 86, 114, 134–6, 141
Ethical, 20, 26, 57, 65–6, 81, 85, 87, 102, 112, 118, 136, 141–2
Ethical considerations, 20, 66, 87, 102, 141
Ethical framework, 57, 141
Ethical issues, 65, 141
Ethical Principles, 112, 141
External, 40, 61, 82, 91, 111, 141
External constraints, 40, 141
External Entity, 91, 141
External influences, 61, 141
Fabricate, 23, 43, 141
Fabricated Laws, 22, 32, 77–9, 116, 141, 144, 146
Manufactured, 15, 20–2, 29, 32, 42–3, 101, 105, 113, 127, 141
Manufactured laws, 15, 21–2, 32, 42–3, 101, 105, 113, 141
Fabrication, 32, 141
Fair, 22, 48, 64, 141
Fair Laws, 48, 141

Fairness, 18, 31, 55, 64, 66–8, 71, 74, 78–9, 82, 141
Fairness and Justice, 71, 82, 141
Fear, 23, 51, 56, 61, 67, 75, 94, 106, 141
Finnis, John, 110, 133, 141–2
Free, 22, 35, 37, 40–2, 47, 61–2, 80, 88, 90–1, 96, 141
Freedom, 3, 17, 20, 29, 39–41, 54, 62, 71, 90–1, 94–100, 107–8, 141, 143
Free will, 35, 37, 40–1, 47, 61–2, 80, 88, 90–1, 96, 141
Functional Changes of Communities, 115–6, 141
Fundamental Rights, 100, 141
Fury of the Divine Creator, 46, 141
Geographical demarcations, 105, 141
Globalized World, 115, 141
God, 4, 15, 26, 45, 111, 141
Good and Proper Order, 110, 141
Government, 3, 138, 141
Government Bodies, 3, 141
Hans Kelsen, 110, 115, 141
Harmony, 27, 97–8, 141, 143
Heavenly Errors, 26, 133, 141
Holders of the Truth, 23, 141
Holistic, 121, 141
Hubris, 23, 141
Human, 1, 3–4, 8, 12–5, 17–24, 26, 29–30, 32, 37–8, 41–3, 45, 47, 49–50, 56, 64, 66, 78–80, 85–8, 90, 93–5, 97, 99–101, 105–6, 108, 110–2, 114–5, 117–8, 122–3, 127, 129–31, 134, 137, 141, 145
Beingness, 1, 141
Human Behavior, 14, 64, 66, 99, 110, 112, 131, 137, 141, 145
Human Beingness, 1, 141
Human emancipation, 42, 141
Human existence, 3, 14, 20–1, 100, 141
Human Freedom, 3, 97, 141
Humanity, 18, 20–1, 30, 43, 114, 141
Human Jurisprudence, 19, 32, 141
Humankind, 24, 30, 105, 111, 123, 141
Human-made, 102, 141
Human Nature, 4, 14, 22, 24, 37–8, 42, 86, 93, 141
Humanness, 21, 141
Human reality, 12, 21–2, 43, 141
Human Reasoning, 85, 87–8, 141

141

Index

Human Rights, 8, 26, 66, 100, 114, 134, 141
Human Spirit, 32, 141
Human unpredictability, 21, 141
Human virtue, 15, 23, 141
Ideal, 39, 42, 51, 64, 73, 97, 117, 127, 141
 Ideal Behavior, 117, 141
 Ideal Conduct, 127, 141
Identity, 30, 32, 46, 96, 141
Implicit Bias, 73, 141
Imposed obligation, 38, 141
Incarceration, 50, 141
Inconsistency, 31, 141
Indisputable State of Being, 29, 141
Individual, 1–2, 4, 7, 9, 12–4, 18–20, 26–30, 37–41, 43, 45–8, 50–1, 54, 56–8, 61–7, 69–75, 80, 86–9, 91, 95–6, 98, 100, 105, 107–8, 110, 117–8, 122–3, 129–30, 141
 Individual Conscience, 86, 141
 Individual liberties, 67, 141
 Individual Reasoning, 129, 141
Induced obedience, 108, 142
Induction, 38, 142
Inevitability, 17, 75, 142
Influence, 3, 26, 31, 40, 46–7, 55–6, 58–9, 62, 65–6, 75, 77, 79, 81, 93–5, 106, 111, 114, 116, 118, 123, 136, 142, 145
Informal Agreement, 27, 142
Inherency, 105, 142
Inherent Obligation, 45–7, 99, 106, 122, 128, 130, 142
Inherent Obligations, 17, 127, 142
Innate Desires, 93, 142
Innate tendencies, 42, 142
Instinct, 18, 93, 101, 142
Institutional Practices, 58, 112, 142
Institutions, 11, 14, 53, 66, 114, 123, 130, 142
Instrumental power, 61–2, 142
Intangible, 55, 59, 96, 142
Intellectual, 12–3, 17, 24–5, 41, 43, 61–2, 80, 90, 97, 99–100, 127, 142
 Intellectual breadth, 43, 142
 Intellectual exploration, 24, 142
 Intellectual Justification for Laws, 80, 142
 Intellectual power, 61–2, 142
International, 8, 14, 106, 134–5, 142
 International laws, 106, 142
Interpersonal, 91, 93, 142

Interpersonal Dynamics, 93, 142
Interpersonal Interactions, 91, 142
Intrinsic, 4, 12–3, 18, 21, 23, 29, 37, 40, 58, 65, 75, 91, 95, 127, 142
 Intrinsic Capriciousness, 29, 142
 Intrinsic Nature, 21, 95, 142
Jeremy Bentham, 112, 142
John Austin, 113–4, 128, 133, 142
John Finnis, 110, 142
Joseph Raz, 11, 118, 128, 134, 142
Jurisprudence, 11, 19, 32, 38–9, 86, 113–4, 119–20, 127, 129–30, 133–4, 136, 138, 141–2, 144
Jurisprudential doctrines, 19, 142
Justice, 11–2, 14, 22, 31, 55, 64–5, 67–8, 71, 74, 82, 85–6, 89, 111, 115, 123, 129, 131, 133, 138, 141–2, 144–5
 Justice and Injustice, 89, 142
Just Laws, 48, 142
Kelsen, Hans, 110–1, 115, 134, 141–2
Law, 1–4, 7–15, 17–23, 25–33, 37–9, 41–3, 46–51, 53–4, 57–82, 85–6, 88–93, 96, 99–102, 105–23, 127–31, 133–46
 Law-abiding Citizen, 50, 107, 142
 Law and Morality, 109, 142
 Law and Order, 71, 142
 Lawbreakers, 107, 142
 Law Enforcement, 3, 11, 31, 50–1, 64–7, 69–75, 77–9, 81–2, 130, 137, 139, 142, 144
  Law enforcement agencies, 65–6, 70, 73, 81–2, 142
  Law Enforcement-Citizen Obedience Dilemma, 78
  Law Enforcement Policies, 69, 142
  Law enforcer, 107, 142
 Laws of Nature, 4, 21–2, 26, 100–1, 109, 115–6, 142
 Law violator, 107, 142
Lawful, 49, 142
Lawmakers, 70, 81, 142
Lawmaking, 111, 142
Legal, 1–4, 8–15, 20–1, 23–5, 27–8, 38–9, 41, 43, 48–9, 51, 53, 57–60, 63–7, 73, 75, 77–82, 86, 88–9, 91, 99, 101, 105–6, 108, 111–22, 128–9, 131, 133–5, 137–8, 142–3, 145
 Legal and Ethical Relationships, 118, 142
 Legal Anthologies, 120, 142
 Legal Authority, 60, 114–5, 142

Legal Chasm, 116, 142
Legal Compliance, 3, 11, 13, 15, 75, 135, 142
Legal Concepts, 119–21, 131, 142
Legal Constructs, 48, 81, 142
Legal Discourse, 28, 142
Legal Doctrine, 3, 101, 113, 120, 142
Legal Dynamics, 121, 142
Legal implications, 24, 142
Legal Inquiry, 119, 128, 142
Legal Intellectuals, 25, 142
Legal norms, 11, 13–4, 59, 65, 67, 75, 142
Legal obedience, 4, 10–4, 20, 38, 80–1, 86, 89, 99, 106, 122, 128, 142, 145
Legal Obligation, 1, 4, 13, 15, 38–9, 48, 57–8, 60, 75, 80, 82, 88, 91, 99, 101, 105–6, 108, 112–3, 117, 119, 122, 128, 131, 134, 142
Legal paradoxes, 23, 142
Legal philosophy, 66, 114, 142
Legal Positivists, 112, 142
Legal power, 63, 142
Legal principles, 9–10, 12, 43, 64, 112, 114, 128, 142
Legal reliance, 21, 142
Legal Repercussions, 51, 143
Legal Rules, 10, 111–2, 128, 143
Legal Structures, 91, 143
Legal system, 39, 65, 75, 78, 81, 121, 143
Legal Systems, 12, 15, 28, 57, 63, 114–5, 119, 128–9, 143, 145
Legal theorists, 108, 117, 143
Legal Theory, 38, 120, 128, 137–8, 143
Legal treatises and doctrines, 9, 143
Legality, 79, 143
Legally, 20, 39, 127, 143
Legally Enforced Rules, 127, 143
Legislation, 2, 11, 49, 129, 137–8, 143
Legislators, 79, 81, 143
Legitimacy, 11–3, 15, 26, 48, 54, 56, 63, 71, 112–3, 119, 136–7, 143
Liberalism, 25, 134, 143
Logical, 18–9, 40, 85, 143
Logical contradiction, 40, 143
Logical Sense, 85, 143
Majority power, 61, 143
Mandate, 1, 12, 63, 143
Man-made, 18, 25, 31, 143
Man-made Laws, 25, 143

Man-made Rules, 31, 143
Maritain, Jacques, 109–10, 135, 143
Materialization, 55, 143
Matrix, 57, 143
Matter, 1, 26, 72, 129, 136
Mechanism, 1, 10, 20, 23, 60, 64, 67, 81, 141, 143
Mechanisms of control, 20, 143
Meeting of the Minds, 27–8, 135, 143
Mental, 11, 17, 27, 42, 46, 61–2, 93–4, 97–8, 110, 143
Mental confinement, 42, 143
Mental Harmony, 27, 143
Mental power, 61–2, 143
Metaphorical, 55, 143
Metaphysical, 98, 143
Metaphysics, 39, 134, 143
Method, 21, 88, 143
Methodology, 21, 112, 119, 143
Misclassification, 32, 143
Misconception, 15, 26, 43, 80, 99, 106, 121, 133, 136, 143
Misguided Worldview, 25, 143
Mistaken Assumptions, 25, 143
Misuse of power, 74, 143
Monopolize, 98, 143
Moral, 11, 13–5, 23, 25, 28, 38, 47–9, 57, 75, 80, 85–7, 99, 109, 111, 113–4, 117, 119–21, 123, 127–30, 134, 136, 138, 143
Moral Compass, 130, 143
Moral Constructs, 85, 143
Moral Dimensions, 127, 143
Moral Duties, 111, 143
Moral Imperatives, 127, 143
Moralists, 12, 143
Morality, 15, 25, 38, 43, 49, 80, 99, 109, 114, 117, 123, 128–9, 134, 142–3
Moral justification, 23, 143
Moral Obligations, 15, 48, 143
Moral Perspectives, 123, 143
Moral Principles, 47–8, 113, 138, 143
Moral Queries, 117, 143
Moral Standards, 86, 143
Moral Theory, 25, 109, 143
Moral Values, 47, 49, 128, 130, 143
Multiplicity in Reasoning, 88
Mutability, 21, 143
Mutual, 28, 72, 98, 115, 118, 143
Mutual Recognition, 118, 143

Index

Mutually, 41, 96, 118, 143
Mutually exclusive, 41, 96, 143
Naturality, 17, 143
Nature, 3–4, 14, 17–8, 20–4, 26–7, 31–2, 37–8, 42, 45, 47–9, 54–6, 60, 66, 73, 77, 79–80, 83, 86–7, 93–8, 100–1, 103, 105–6, 108–11, 113, 115–6, 119, 122–3, 128–9, 131, 133, 139, 141–4, 146
  Natural, 3–5, 13, 17–8, 20–2, 25–7, 29–33, 37–9, 42–3, 47, 80, 85, 88, 93–102, 105, 107–18, 120, 123, 127–30, 133–6, 138, 140, 143
    Natural environment, 17, 94, 101, 115, 143
    Natural Freedom, 94, 99, 143
    Natural Law, 3–4, 17, 22, 25–6, 29, 31–3, 43, 80, 85, 88, 99–101, 105, 108–18, 123, 127, 129–30, 133–6, 138, 143
    Natural Law Theories, 85, 143
    Natural order, 18, 105, 143
    Natural Reason, 85, 143
    Natural rights, 107, 110, 133, 138, 143
    Natural state, 29, 38, 47, 94, 143
  Nature and Society, 31, 143
  Nature of Obedience, 17, 66, 131, 143
Negotiation, 9, 67, 135, 144
Noncompliance, 2, 39, 50, 60, 89, 144
Non-Consent, 28, 133, 144
Nonenforcement, 39, 144
Nonexistent, 98, 123, 144
Nonnatural, 93, 144
Nonnegotiable, 2, 31, 72, 144
Nonsensical, 91, 144
Norm, 11–4, 27, 45, 47–9, 57–9, 61–8, 73, 75, 80, 86–7, 91–2, 95, 98–9, 112, 117–8, 122, 127–31, 135, 139–40, 142, 144–5
  Normative, 28, 117–9, 135–6, 144
    Normative Consent, 28, 135–6, 144
    Normative Law, 117, 144
  Norms and Values, 47, 63, 80, 99, 122, 127, 144
Nuanced World of Jurisprudence, 129, 144
Obey, 3, 10–5, 20, 26, 37–9, 46, 50–1, 65, 72–3, 75–6, 89, 101, 105, 107, 118, 122–3, 128, 130, 134, 136, 140, 144

Obedient, 32, 130, 144
  Obedience, 1–5, 10–5, 17, 20, 23–4, 26–31, 37–9, 41, 43, 46, 48–51, 53, 58–62, 65–7, 73, 75–82, 86, 89, 91, 99, 105–6, 108–9, 120–3, 128, 130–1, 134–5, 139, 142–5
  Obedience and Conformity, 29, 144
Objective Injustice, 115–6, 144
Obligation, 1–4, 7–15, 17–8, 20, 28, 31–3, 37–43, 45–8, 50, 53, 57–8, 60, 72, 75, 80, 82, 86–9, 91–3, 96, 99, 101, 103, 105–6, 108, 112–3, 117–23, 127–31, 133–5, 137–8, 141–6
Obligation Theory, 38, 144
Offender, 26, 72, 136, 144
Ontological, 31, 94, 144
Outlaw, 107–8, 144
Overpower, 54, 144
Overreach, 82, 144
Override, 28, 144
Paradox, 21, 23, 42, 77–8, 87, 96, 142, 144
  Paradox of Laws, 78, 144
Paternalistic, 18, 144
Penalties, 60, 75, 107, 144
Person, 2, 4, 18–20, 26–8, 42, 72–4, 87–9, 95, 100, 107, 109–10, 130, 144
  Personal, 20, 40–1, 46, 56, 61–2, 64, 75, 81, 87, 89, 91, 130, 144
    Personal autonomy, 20, 144
    Personal Benefits, 89, 144
    Personal desires, 40, 144
    Personality, 14, 18, 136, 144
    Personal Responsibility, 91, 144
  Personify, 53, 144
Philosophy, 11, 13, 28, 38, 66, 109–12, 114, 117, 134, 137–8, 142, 144
Physical power, 58, 61–2, 144
Police, 3, 11, 13, 53–4, 58–9, 69–70, 72–3, 108, 144
  Police Authority, 3, 144
  Police force, 53, 59, 144
Political, 11, 14, 28, 48, 62, 80–1, 89, 92, 99, 117, 119–21, 133, 137–8, 144
  Political Discourse, 117, 121, 144
  Political Obligation, 11, 14, 80, 89, 92, 99, 137–8, 144
Positive, 2, 4, 18, 25, 32, 80, 93, 99–101, 111–7, 120, 122–3, 127–30, 140, 144

Positive Law, 2, 4, 25, 32, 80, 93, 99–101, 111–7, 120, 122–3, 127–30, 140, 144
  Positivist, 38, 112, 142, 144
  Positivism, 111, 144
Power, 3–4, 40, 47, 51, 53–67, 69–74, 79–81, 96, 98, 108, 118, 122–3, 140, 142–5
  Power Dynamics, 55, 62, 66, 69–70, 72, 144
  Power of Suggestion, 122, 144
  Power of the Law, 61, 144
Practical, 25, 80, 88, 110, 119, 144
  Practical Application, 119, 144
  Practical Dimensions, 25, 144
  Practical Reason, 88, 144
  Practical Right-Mindedness, 110, 144
Precocity of Fabricated Laws, 77–8, 144
Predictability, 21, 64, 144
Primal instincts, 42, 144
Principle of Justice, 115, 144
Professionalism, 65, 144
Prone to Obedience, 20, 26, 144
Protection from Law Enforcers, 51, 144
Prudence, 88, 144
Psychological Maturation, 30, 144
Public Affairs, 130, 144
Public Trust in Law Enforcement, 69–71, 144
Punishment, 32, 50, 58–9, 75, 107, 139, 144
Punitive Consequences, 50, 144
Racial Profiling, 69–70, 72–3, 144
Racism, 49, 144
Rational, 1–2, 18, 46, 87, 90, 105, 144
  Rationality, 2, 13, 19, 85–6, 144
  Rational nature, 18, 105, 144
  Rational Thinker, 2, 144
Raymond Wacks, 109, 119, 145
Raz, Joseph, 11, 118, 128, 134, 136, 142, 145
Reality, 2–3, 12, 20–3, 29, 31–2, 40, 42–3, 46, 51, 54, 58, 65–6, 70, 76, 78, 90, 94–6, 117, 121, 123, 127, 131, 141, 145
Reason, 1–2, 18, 22, 26, 28, 38–9, 45–7, 50, 70, 83, 85–91, 97, 106, 109–10, 117, 122, 127, 136, 140, 143–5
  Reasonable Creatures, 86, 145
Regulating Conducts, 90, 145

Regulation, 3, 10, 21, 62, 66, 69, 72, 74–5, 78, 81, 105–6, 111, 139–40, 145
Religious, 42, 45, 62, 114, 145
  Religious Beliefs, 114, 145
  Religious predispositions, 42, 145
Relinquish, 29, 80, 95, 145
Repercussions, 2, 51, 54, 56, 59, 72, 75, 81, 107, 143, 145
Responsibilities, 8–9, 58, 64–5, 145
Restraint, 54, 145
Restriction, 41, 96, 99, 145
Right, 3, 8, 26–7, 29, 39, 41, 45, 49, 64–7, 69–74, 77, 85–6, 91, 100, 106–7, 109–11, 114–5, 118, 133–4, 138–9, 141, 143, 145
  Righteousness, 49, 51, 75, 122, 128, 130, 145
  Right-mindedness, 110, 144–5
  Rights-Based, 28, 134, 145
Rule, 3, 10, 20, 23, 27, 31, 37–8, 48–50, 61, 63–4, 66–8, 74–6, 111–2, 114, 116, 123, 127–8, 131, 140, 143, 145
  Rule of Law, 48, 63–4, 66–8, 74–6, 145
  Rules and Regulations, 3, 111, 145
Scholarly Literature, 1, 145
Sectarian power, 61–2, 145
Secularism, 57, 145
Secular Legal Systems, 114, 145
Selective Legal Obedience, 81, 145
Selective Obedience, 79, 81–2, 145
Self, 2, 4, 18, 20, 28, 30, 57, 91, 145
  Secular, 114, 145
  Self-defined, 23, 145
  Self-induced Obligation, 2, 145
  Self-Subordination, 93, 145
  Self-worth, 30, 145
Self-control, 4, 145
Self-determination, 39–40, 145
Sense of Duty, 29, 46–7, 145
Shared norms, 63, 145
Social, 1, 3, 8, 10, 13–4, 19–20, 22, 26–8, 30, 37, 39, 42, 45–50, 56–9, 62, 64, 66, 74–5, 85–7, 89, 92, 94–9, 101, 107, 112, 116, 118–9, 123, 129–31, 134–7, 145
  Social compliance, 19, 145
  Social condemnation, 107, 145
  Social Construct, 94, 130, 145
  Social context, 37, 66, 94, 96–7, 101, 119, 131, 145

Social Contract, 28, 75, 99, 145
Social Environment, 1, 27, 89, 94, 99, 145
Social Expectations, 75, 131, 145
Social Groups, 123, 129, 145
Social Interaction, 30, 58, 118, 145
Social Justice, 74, 145
Social Laws, 46, 99, 123, 129–30, 145
Social Networks, 26, 136, 145
Social Norms, 27, 47–9, 58, 66, 75, 86, 92, 98–9, 112, 130–1, 135, 145
Social order, 22, 58–9, 62, 64, 75, 96, 130, 145
Social Reason, 85, 145
Social Rules, 48, 131, 145
Social structures, 20, 42, 56–7, 116, 123, 145
Socially Imposed Duty, 2, 145
Societal, 12, 27, 45, 47, 55, 61–2, 67, 72–3, 75, 79–80, 85–7, 91, 95–8, 105, 121–2, 129–30, 140, 145
Societal Aspirations, 130, 145
Societal Confines, 86, 145
Societal construct, 105, 145
Societal Influence, 95, 145
Societal Norms, 12, 47, 61, 73, 86, 91, 95, 129–30, 145
Societal Values, 67, 129, 145
Socioeconomic, 71, 145
Socioeconomic Status, 71, 145
Sociopolitical, 81, 127, 145
Soft force, 58–60, 145
Sovereignty, 99, 138, 145
Standard for Human Behavior, 110, 145
State of Purity, 30, 145
Statute, 49–50, 64, 66, 78, 145
Stereotyping, 73, 145
Stop and Frisk Program, 69
Subhuman, 100, 145
Subjective, 32, 77–8, 145
Subjectivity, 31, 79, 89, 145
Subjugation, 46, 106, 145
Submission, 20, 74, 94, 146
Submissive, 4, 94, 146
Subordination, 94, 146
Supreme truth, 42, 146
Survival Strategies, 93, 146

Symbolism of Law Representation, 51, 146
Synthetic Laws, 2, 21–2, 30, 32, 48, 77, 111, 146
Tangible, 19, 22, 54–6, 58–60, 63, 78, 97, 146
Taxation, 4, 146
Taxes, 99, 146
Temporal and spatial contexts, 19, 146
The Fickleness of Men, 21, 146
The Nature of Fabricated Laws, 77, 146
Theology, 123, 138, 146
Theoretical, 11, 25, 37, 119, 129, 146
Transparency, 31, 64–5, 71, 81, 146
Truth, 23, 29, 35, 41–3, 45, 79, 81, 95, 141, 146
Ultimate truth, 35, 41, 43, 146
Unambiguous Acknowledgment, 29, 146
Unconditional obligation, 42, 146
Unconstrained, 17, 89, 146
Universal, 2, 25, 32, 85, 87–90, 100, 110, 114, 119, 128, 131, 146
Universal Laws, 128, 146
Universal Mode of Conduct, 90, 146
Universal Percept, 25, 146
Universal Application, 2, 146
Universe, 21, 26, 133, 146
Validation, 27, 140, 146
Validity, 95, 146
Values, 8, 10, 47–51, 63–4, 67, 80, 99, 112, 115, 117, 122–3, 127–31, 133, 140, 143–6
Varying Perspectives, 121, 146
Violation, 7, 28, 39, 59, 69–71, 78–9, 136, 146
Virtuous Conduct, 118, 146
Vital Forces, 115–6, 146
Voluntary act, 43–4, 146
Whimsical, 19, 28, 32, 77–8, 146
Wilderness, 89, 146
Wisdom, 30, 42, 87, 146
Worldly, 45, 146
Worldview, 4, 18–9, 25, 40, 43, 143, 146
Wrong, 41, 85–6, 106, 110–1, 115, 146
Wrongful, 118, 146

www.ingramcontent.com/pod-product-compliance
Lightning Source LLC
Chambersburg PA
CBHW031958080426
42735CB00007B/438